THE OTHER
1492

Kathy as Fred —
Another chapter in our history

Mom and Pop

NORMAN H. FINKELSTEIN

THE OTHER
1492

JEWISH SETTLEMENT IN THE NEW WORLD

Beech Tree Books, New York

Charles Scribner's Sons Books for Young Readers
Macmillan Publishing Company
866 Third Avenue, New York, NY 10022
Collier Macmillan Canada, Inc.

Printed in the United States of America
First Beech Tree Edition, 1992.
10 9 8 7 6 5 4 3 2 1

Library of Congress Cataloging-in-Publication Data
Finkelstein, Norman H.
The other 1492: Jewish settlement in the new world/
Norman H. Finkelstein—1st ed.
p.   cm.   Bibliography: p.   Includes index.
Summary: Describes the causes, events, and aftermath
of the expulsion of the Jews from Spain in 1492.
1. Jews—Spain—History—Juvenile literature.
2. Sephardim—History—Juvenile literature.
3. Spain—Ethnic relations—Juvenile literature.
[1. Jews—Spain—History.   2. Sephardim—History.
3. Spain—Ethnic relations.]   I. Title.
DS135.S7F47 1989   946'.004924—dc20   89—6253 CIP AC
ISBN 0-688-11572-1

For My Children
Jeffrey, Robert, and Risa

Acknowledgments

The author wishes to thank the following for their assistance: Dr. Maurice Tuchman, Librarian, and the staff of the Hebrew College Library, Brookline, Massachusetts. Dr. Janice Etzkowitz, Executive Director of Congregation Shearith Israel in the City of New York. Bernard Wax, Director, and Dr. Nathan Kaganoff, Librarian, of the American Jewish Historical Society, Waltham, Massachusetts. Rabbi Jerry Schwartzbard and the staff of the Jewish Theological Seminary Library, New York. Mr. Ion de la Riva of the Comisión Nacional Quinto Centenario, Madrid, Spain. My wife, Rosalind, for her advice and unending patience.

Contents

THE OTHER
1492

ONE

Expulsion and Exploration

"Within three months there must not remain in my kingdom a single Jew."

KING FERDINAND OF SPAIN

In the spring of 1492, within a three-week period, King Ferdinand and Queen Isabella of Spain issued two seemingly unrelated but fateful decrees. In the first, issued on March 31, 1492, the royal couple ordered all Jews to leave Spanish soil within four months; they could take nothing of value with them. The second edict, on April 17, bestowed the exalted title Admiral of the Ocean Sea upon a persistent Genoese sailor, Christopher Columbus, and directed him to undertake an expedition in search of a new route to the rich Indies.

That spring and summer the expulsion order attracted wide attention. Throughout Spain, Jewish families were busily winding up their affairs, saying tearful good-byes, and making plans for their departures. The plight of the Jews affected nearly every Spanish vil-

1

lage: no one could ignore the upheaval. Even Columbus, whose thoughts were now intently focused on his upcoming voyage, began the diary of his momentous journey by noting what was happening to the Jews. "In the same month," he wrote, "in which Their Majesties issued the edict that all Jews should be driven out of their kingdoms and territories, in the same month, they gave me the order to undertake, with sufficient men, my expedition to the Indies."

There are some scholars who suggest that Columbus himself may have had Jewish roots. Whether this is true or not, there is no doubt that Columbus knew many Jews and that his celebrated voyage was made possible by their contributions and efforts. The noted astronomer Abraham Zacuto designed the astronomical charts that assured Columbus a safe voyage. Important Jewish mapmakers, like the Crescas brothers, were much sought after by other explorers of the time. Among the ships' crews were at least three Jews including Luis de Torres, the interpreter. He became the first European to set foot upon the soil of the New World because of his knowledge of Hebrew and Arabic, languages Columbus thought the natives of the Indies would probably speak.

Columbus first attempted to secure Ferdinand and Isabella's support in 1486. Although they expressed interest in his plan at the time, a commitment was not forthcoming. The monarchs were involved in a prolonged and costly war to wrest the last piece of Spanish soil from the Moslems who had ruled parts of the country for centuries. With the fall of Granada to the Catholic forces early in 1492, all of Spain was in Christian hands. Now other affairs of state could be considered.

During those intervening years, support at the royal court for Columbus and his plan had come from two important Jewish advisers to the king and queen, Luis de Santangel and Don Isaac Abravanel. Santangel, the royal treasurer, was a Marrano—that is, a baptized Jew who in public behaved like a Christian but inwardly considered himself still a Jew. *Marranos*, the Spanish word for pigs, was the contemptuous term given these "New Christians" by the established Catholics, and the name has endured. The traditional Jewish community maintained cordial relations with the Marranos, however, and in later years, when given the opportunity, many returned to their original Jewish faith.

There were many like Santangel in Spain: Jews whose families over the years had been forced to renounce their own faith and accept Catholicism. Many New Christians advanced quickly in professions not previously open to them as Jews. By 1492 many of their descendents had reached the highest positions available in government, business, and even the Church. It was said there was hardly an aristocratic family in all of Spain—including the king's—that did not have at least a little Jewish blood flowing in its veins.

Don Isaac Abravanel had not renounced his faith. He was, in fact, a respected Jewish scholar and the author of several biblical commentaries. He had helped, in large measure, to finance Ferdinand and Isabella's war to recapture Granada.

Both Santangel and Abravanel saw beyond the immediate benefits to the monarchy of a successful voyage by Columbus. They realized the tremendous implications the settlement of a new land had for the increasingly harassed Jews of Spain. Knowing that the royal treasury was greatly depleted because of the long war, they even offered to finance the voyage themselves. Their lengthy behind-the-scenes maneuvering finally paid off when the monarchs granted Columbus permission and funds to sail. The stature of these two men at court could not, however, prevent the Catholic Majesties, as Ferdinand and Isabella were called, from ordering the expulsion of all the Jews from Spain.

The move toward expulsion had begun in 1480, as the cen-

A painting depicting Christopher Columbus at the royal court of Spain. *Courtesy Library of Congress.*

turies-long Moslem rule in Spain was coming to an end. In order to secure Spain as a totally Catholic country, Ferdinand and Isabella instituted an Inquisition, a court of inquiry, to enforce strict religious standards for all Catholics in Spain, especially the highly suspect New Christians. The chief inquisitor was a zealous monk, Tomás de Torquemada.

Under the law, the Inquisition was prohibited from conducting its work among professing Jews. Only the already baptized were subject to inquiry. Some accounts estimate that at the time the Inquisition was instituted, nearly one-half of all Spanish Jews had converted to Christianity. They may not have been firmly rooted in their Jewish faith, but neither were all of them loyal Christians. While they attended church regularly, at home they secretly lit Sabbath candles, refrained from eating pork, and observed the Jewish High Holy Days. Although Torquemada did what he could to root out less than sincere Marranos, he saw the professing Jews as the real enemy. They, after all, provided comfort and a sense of tradition for many Marranos. He would not rest until he had succeeded in banishing all the Jews from Spain.

Even the highly religious Ferdinand and Isabella at first found it difficult to accept Torquemada's plan. The Jews were among the most successful merchants, bankers, and scholars in the country. Even at the court, Jewish and Marrano advisors like Santangel and Abravanel were highly respected. To drive the Jews out would cause great hardship to the entire nation. But Torquemada was a patient man and for years he hammered his message of hate into the minds of the king and queen.

With the royal couple on the verge of giving in to Torquemada's bigoted obsession, Don Isaac Abravanel approached their majesties one final time. He implored them not to end nearly fifteen centuries of Jewish life in Spain. Promising them all manner of wealth, Don Isaac literally begged them to reconsider. Finally, as a last resort, he offered the entirety of his own fortune of thirty thousand gold ducats—a truly regal ransom. King Ferdinand, who until now had shown no reaction to Don Isaac's pleadings, suddenly became attentive.

But the fate of the Jews was already sealed. Unknown to the monarchs, Torquemada had been listening at the door. As the king appeared to waver at Don Isaac's proposal, the infuriated monk burst into the royal chamber waving a crucifix wildly in the air. "Behold the crucified whom the accursed Judas Iscariot sold for thirty pieces of silver," he screamed. "Your majesties are about to sell him for thirty thousand ducats. Here he is. Take him and sell him!" Thereupon the enraged Torquemada flung the crucifix in the faces of the monarchs, turned, and rushed from the room.

Whatever seeds of doubt Abravanel had planted in the mind of the king vanished in the shock of that moment. On March 31, 1492, Ferdinand and Isabella issued the expulsion order. Four months later, the Jews were streaming toward the port cities of Spain to begin their uncertain futures as exiles. Among them, giving encouragement and hope, was Don Isaac Abravanel.

A number of Jews chose to accept baptism as a way of remaining in the only homeland they had ever known. Two hundred thousand others left Spain forever, unable to understand what had happened to their world. The last Jew left Spain on August 2, 1492. A day later Columbus and his hardy crew sailed out of the harbor at Palos. As the admiral and his three ships headed toward their place in history, Jews in other ships wondered if they would ever find a secure home.

Some of the Jewish refugees turned to Portugal and a temporary haven, the Inquisition close on their heels. Others sailed to Italy, Holland, Turkey, and those Mediterranean ports that would accept them. The Turkish sultan, knowing how they had enriched the Spanish nation, made them particularly welcome and looked forward to the same good fortune.

Many Jews and Marranos ultimately made their way to South America, in the New World which Columbus had discovered. There, they hoped to place themselves as far away from the Inquisi-

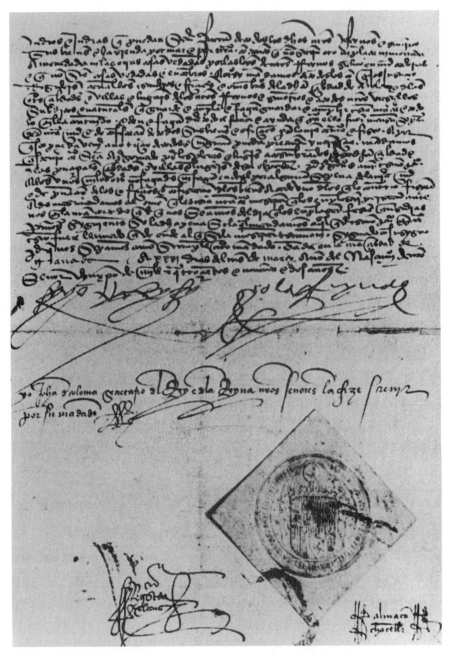

The Edict of Expulsion signed by King Ferdinand and Queen Isabella of Spain at Granada on March 31, 1492. *Courtesy Beth Hatefutsoth, The Nahum Goldmann Museum of the Jewish Diaspora, Israel.*

tion as possible. In time, however, the Inquisition followed them across the Atlantic and Jews again found themselves on the move. In 1654 twenty-three refugees from Recife, Brazil, became the first Jewish settlers in a land that would later be known as the United States of America. Here they and their fellow coreligionists would at last find the freedoms and liberties that had been denied them in their "golden Spain."

TWO

The Golden Age

"My heart is in the east and I in the uttermost west."

JUDAH HALEVI (1086–1145)

The expulsion from Spain was not the first experience of its kind for the Jews. Rooted in Jewish history is a long and sad tradition of forced movements. Once, the Jews had a land of their own. Whether known as Canaan, Israel, Palestine, or the Holy Land, this piece of earth has had an importance to Jews that was not only historical but religious and emotional. Even when physically separated from that land, for short or long periods, Jews never allowed themselves to forget their ancient homeland.

We learn from history about many peoples who were conquered by stronger neighbors and then disappeared from the face of the earth. But unlike the Edomites, Sumerians, and Phoenicians, the Jews survived. Each new threat to survival only served to strengthen the Jews' attachment to their religion, culture, and land.

In 586 B.C. the mighty Babylonian army sacked the city of

Jerusalem and reduced the Holy Temple of the Jewish people to ashes. The political, religious, and educational leaders of Jewish society were forced from their country and taken as captives to Babylon. There by the rivers of Babylon, they consoled themselves with the hope that their exile would soon be over. Forty-five years passed before they were allowed to return. By that time most Jews had accommodated themselves to the stylish and comfortable life outside the Holy Land and only a small, dedicated group undertook the difficult journey back. The rest established a Jewish life for themselves in Babylon while retaining close ties with their homeland. This pattern was followed by later generations of Jews, including those who settled in Europe.

The scene was now set in Palestine for a new era in which Jewish government would be heavily dependent on foreign powers for survival. First the Greeks and then the Romans exerted their political and military influence. It was only when foreign powers tried to impose religious controls over Jewish beliefs that the people rebelled.

As the power of Rome grew, increased friction led to a series of disastrous revolts by the Jews. In A.D. 70 the city of Jerusalem was captured by the Romans and the Second Temple was destroyed. By A.D. 132 a final desperate revolt had failed miserably and the Romans had destroyed the entire city of Jerusalem. For the second time in Jewish history the Temple, Judaism's central focus and authority, was gone; this time it would not be rebuilt. Unlike the first exile, which lasted less than fifty years, this one was to last nearly two thousand, until 1948.

Building upon the lessons of the first exile in Babylon, the Jews adapted their religion to the absence of the Holy Temple in Jerusalem. But wherever they went, they could not forget Jerusalem.

Indeed, there is a commemorative day in the Jewish calendar, Tisha b'Av (the ninth day of the Jewish month of Av), that marks the exact day and month on which both Holy Temples were destroyed. Centuries later, that same day and month in 1492 would mark the expulsion of the last Jews from Spain.

When they were driven out of their land by the Romans during the first century, the Jews began a new and long chapter in their history. Their two-thousand-year exile from Palestine scattered the Jewish people to the four corners of the earth and is known as the Diaspora, from the Greek word for dispersion.

A large number of exiles went to Babylonia, where communities of Jews, descended from the time of the first exile, were already living. There they established important centers of learning to which Jews in other lands turned for religious guidance. The Talmud, the highly detailed and important interpretation of biblical law, was organized and established during this period. Moreover, the synagogue was strengthened as the new center of Jewish religious and communal life. These two innovations allowed Jews, no matter where they lived, to continue their religious practices without Palestine and a Holy Temple.

Other Jews were taken to Rome as captives, while yet others made their way to cities along the Mediterranean that were under Roman control. Within a few generations there were established Jewish communities in a number of European cities, mainly in the West, including Spain.

Looking for places to live where they might find safety, Jews moved into northern areas of Europe by the year 800. But no matter where they settled, after a period of time they were usually forced to move on because of religious intolerance.

As Christianity grew to become the national religion of the Ro-

An engraving recalls the expulsion of the Jews from Frankfurt, Germany, in 1614. *Courtesy New York Public Library Picture Collection.*

man Empire, the effect on the Jews of Europe became increasingly negative. Jews were accused of having killed Jesus and were looked upon with suspicion and hatred wherever they settled. Over the centuries they lived under many discriminatory laws throughout Christian Europe.

Only in Spain were things different. Although Spanish Church leaders sometimes legislated anti-Jewish laws, these were largely ignored. In fact, the Jews and their non-Jewish neighbors lived in relative peace and harmony. The early Spanish Jews were land-owners, merchants, and government officials. They easily adapted their lives to the fast-changing political and economic conditions of the times. Even as the Roman Empire crumbled and Spain was overrun by the Vandals and Visigoths, Jews were able to maintain peaceful relations with the new rulers.

But as Jewish history has shown, even the most peaceful situations do not last. In 589 the Visigoth king Reccared converted to Christianity and under the influence of Church leaders issued an edict that, in effect, banned Judaism from the country. Jews were given the choice of converting to Christianity or leaving Spain. Although there were harsh times, this law was not strictly enforced because the Visigoths depended on Jewish businesses to keep the kingdom economically alive. Only under the rule of King Sisebut (612–621) did conditions for the Jews become particularly difficult. Many converted or left Spain for nearby northern Africa.

In the year 711, when the Moslems invaded Spain, a new era of tolerance began for all Spaniards. For the Jews especially, the next five hundred years would lovingly and, later, longingly be known as the golden age.

The massive invasion of the Moslems, or Moors, as they were called, across the Mediterranean from North Africa turned much of Spain into an Arab state, Al-Andalus. Only in the north of Spain were a few small Christian kingdoms allowed to exist. In time, these Christian enclaves grew stronger and by the year 1100 their rulers were making a significant start in the "Reconquest" of Spain from the Moors.

Meanwhile, Islamic traditions became interwoven with Spanish culture. Arab civilization was relatively advanced and the con-

13

querors brought with them highly developed skills in mathematics, science, philosophy, and medicine.

For the thousands of Jews who entered Spain with the Moors and for those already in Spain who could now shed their forcible conversions to Christianity, life was pleasant and productive. Jews became involved in all aspects of Spanish life and in large measure served as "middlemen" between the Arab and Christian cultures. Jews played an important role in the Toledo School of Translators. It was common practice for Jewish scholars in Moorish Spain to translate Arabic books into Hebrew, which their counterparts in the Christian north would then translate into Spanish or Latin. At the same time these scholars continued to support Jewish learning and tradition.

The early rule of the Moors was marked by constant political and military skirmishing. Not until Abd-al-Rahman III (912–961) became caliph, or ruler, was a unified Moslem kingdom established, with its seat of power in Cordova. It was during his rule that Hasdai ibn Shaprut (925–975) became the first Jew in Moorish Spain to attain prominence. Although other Jews had served in the courts of previous caliphs, none achieved the success or fame of Hasdai.

A physician to the caliph, Hasdai possessed other skills as well. His knowledge of languages proved to be of great help in the diplomatic area and Hasdai soon found himself at the heart of many foreign-policy decisions. He became a trusted and influential adviser to the caliph and used that position of power to assure the safety and well-being of his fellow Jews.

He is also credited with establishing a major Talmudic academy in Cordova where Spanish Jews developed their own religious traditions independent of the existing centers of learning in Babylonia. In effect, Hasdai laid the groundwork for the creation of an original Jewish life-style based on age-old traditions influenced by the Spanish experience. This bridging of the worlds of secular learning and religion became a model for Jewish life in other countries.

Jewish learning existed side by side with secular learning. Young Jews studied mathematics, philosophy, and the sciences as well as Hebrew grammar and the Talmud, the writings that elaborate on Jewish religious traditions and civil law.

It was the practice in those days for Jewish communities to pay the ransom of fellow Jews abducted by pirates on the open seas. One day such a ransomed Jew was found sitting at the rear of the academy in Cordova. First hesitatingly and then persuasively, he began answering complex religious questions with such brilliance that the learned head of the academy resigned on the spot and turned the position of leadership over to him. The newcomer was Moses ben Hanoch, formerly a respected teacher at a Babylonian academy. Now, with Hasdai's financial and political backing and his own scholarly reputation, Moses brought Spain the prestige of a first-rate center for Jewish scholarship.

Another important personage of that period was Samuel ibn Naghdela (993–1056). When political unrest among the Moslem factions in Cordova resulted in a civil war, Samuel moved to Granada and opened a grocer's shop near the palace gates. His reputation as a man knowledgeable in languages and writing quickly spread among court officials. Soon, many of the lower palace staff began calling upon him to compose their official letters.

In a short time, the grand vizier, chief adviser to the king, learned of the talented grocer and appointed the young man his secretary. Samuel performed his duties with great wisdom and upon the death of the vizier was appointed in his place. In a strange shift of responsibilities, Samuel, the former grocer, now found himself, as grand vizier, at the head of the king's armies.

After planning and leading a series of successful battles, Samuel earned a reputation as a brilliant commander. His accomplishments as second in command to the king contributed to the growth and security of the Jewish community in Granada. The king later appointed him Nagid, or leader of the Jews, in which position Samuel supported the spread of Jewish learning throughout Spain and the Near East.

Leaders like Samuel ha Nagid and Hasdai ibn Shaprut highlight the contributions Jewish people made to Spanish society, but it was the work of the poets and philosophers that left a more lasting imprint upon the Jewish people.

Solomon ibn Gabirol (1021–1069) and Moses ibn Ezra (1080–1139) were among the foremost Jewish poets of their time. They wrote widely about the life of Spanish Jews and about religion. Solomon wrote in both Hebrew and Arabic. His *The Fountains of Faith* became a much-revered work on the fundamentals of religious faith and for centuries was studied by Catholic monks in Latin translation.

The religious thoughts of these poets were marked by a universality that was typical of the Moorish society in which they flourished. That universality became a characteristic of Spanish Jewry. One could be true to one's religion and traditions while actively contributing to the world at large.

Perhaps the greatest of the Jewish poets was Judah Halevi (1086–1145). Although a noted physician and a member of upper-class society, he yearned with a burning passion for the ancient Jewish homeland in Palestine. To him the Jewish presence in Spain or anywhere else in the Diaspora was but a temporary escape. "My heart is in the east," he sadly wrote, "and I in the uttermost west."

The beautiful poetry of all three men found its way into the Jewish Prayer Book. Even today, their messages of hope and faith

A painting showing the observance of the Sabbath in a Jewish home in Spain during the tenth and eleventh centuries. *Courtesy Beth Hatefutsoth, The Nahum Goldmann Museum of the Jewish Diaspora, Israel.*

are as meaningful as when they were written under the Spanish sun.

The foremost Spanish Jew was Moses ben Maimon, known as Maimonides (1135–1204). Like many Jewish intellectuals of the time, he was a physician, but while he made important contributions to the practice of medicine, his greatest accomplishments were in the study of philosophy and religion.

Moses ben Maimon was born in Cordova. A few weeks after his

17

Bar Mitzvah in 1148, he and his family were forced to leave Spain because of an invasion of fanatical Arabs. These new Moslem rulers were not as tolerant as the earlier Arab invaders, and many Jewish families fled for their lives. Some made their way to the quickly growing Christian kingdoms in northern Spain. Others, like the Maimon family, wandered through North Africa. The young Moses, who received a varied education in the sciences and Jewish religion, settled in Egypt. There he served as physician to the royal court of Saladin and, at the same time, as rabbi to the Jews of Cairo. He wrote extensively on secular and religious topics.

As the reputation of Moses ben Maimon grew, Jewish communities around the world turned to him for advice on religious matters. Within a short time, he became the single most important individual in the Jewish world. "From Moses until Moses there has been none like Moses," it was said. Quite an honor if one considers the reputations of numerous other Jewish scholars throughout the centuries! His commentaries on Jewish law and philosophy have become an integral part of the Jewish tradition.

Maimonides was a product of his time, and his writing and thinking reflect this. As a physician and worldly intellectual, he brought to his religious writing an outlook that reflected the multicultural world in which he lived. His *Guide to the Perplexed* provided the Jews of the time with an understanding of how to accept religious faith in a "modern" age. His *Mishneh Torah* provided Jews with an easy-to-follow guide to Jewish law and observance. A good example of his liberal outlook was his attitude toward those Jews forced to convert to the Moslem religion. He understood their pain and did not chastise them, as other rabbis did. Instead, he urged them to be strong and secretly practice Judaism as well as they could.

The universal contributions of Maimonides are today widely recognized. In Cordova a prominent statue of the physician-scholar stands in a courtyard in the old Jewish Quarter. To honor the 850th anniversary of his birth, countries around the world, led by Spain, held special observances and issued postage stamps bearing his likeness.

The Golden Age of the Jews in Spain was an unprecedented time. While it was not perfect—and indeed had its own periods of discrimination, expulsion, and forced conversion—this five-hundred-year period allowed Jews to become active participants in the country's political, social, and business life. At the same time, their own religious culture and learning were enriched by the cosmopolitan society surrounding them. Whether under Arab or Christian rule, life for Spanish Jews was considerably better than that experienced by other European Jews. All this was now to change for the worse.

By 1248, as the northern Catholic kingdoms continued their successful but bloody reconquest of Spain, the Moors were pushed back into the kingdom of Granada. Although that last Moorish kingdom would not be recaptured until 1492, most Spanish soil was now in the hands of Christians. Sadly for the Jews, this unification signaled the beginning of the end of their long presence in Spain. The brutal anti-Semitism that was so much a part of life in other European countries would now hit Golden Spain with a vengeance.

THREE

New Christians, Old Troubles

"All this was love of pillage and plunder rather than devotion."

PEDRO LOPEZ DE AYALA, 1391

The Reconquest, which began in the eleventh century, gave the people of Spain new pride in themselves, their land, and their religion. Yet it was also a time of great disunity. Political and economic problems between Spanish kingdoms were often settled on bloody battlefields. Moreover, Granada was still under Moorish control.

Even as Christian life renewed itself, Spaniards began to take increasing notice of their highly visible Jewish neighbors. The Jews of Spain were represented in all the professions, and served as financial advisers at many royal courts. Their value to royalty was rewarded by the protection they generally received from the kings. But the success of the Jews only called attention to the fact that they differed religiously and culturally from the Catholic majority. In time, jealousy and bigotry overtook the Jews of Spain.

Wild and false rumors about Jews and their religion spread throughout the countryside. The Jews, it was said, stole Christian children and used their blood in religious rituals. Some even believed Jews poisoned wells as a way to kill good Christians.

By the middle of the fourteenth century local governments and the Church enacted new laws against Jews. Although the laws were not always obeyed, violence against Jews became commonplace. Most attacks were incited by religious fanatics but carried out by street mobs bent only on rape and plunder. In 1355 nearly twelve hundred Jews were killed in Toledo when their homes were savagely attacked. Similar attacks occurred in other Spanish cities.

In 1371 King Henry II decreed that Jews had to wear distinctive badges on their clothing and could no longer have Christian names. In some areas, Jews were not allowed to associate with Christians and were restricted to special residential quarters called Juderias. In some places they were not permitted to build new synagogues and were even prevented from appearing in public on the Christian holy day of Good Friday.

Since the days of Maimonides conditions within the Jewish community had worsened both materially and morally. The golden age was long gone. Within the Juderias, poverty was common and many Jews slowly turned away from the scholarship and religious practices of their fathers.

The values of the community also changed for the worse. In one celebrated incident Joseph Pichon, a Jewish tax collector for King Henry II, was executed as a result of false testimony given by jealous fellow Jews. His death continued to fuel bad feeling against Jews in general.

In June 1391, mobs in Seville went on a terrible rampage. Continual preaching by Fernan Martinez, the archdeacon of Ecija, incited the anti-Jewish violence. "Spain for Christians," the mobs shouted. Homes in the Jewish quarter were robbed, burned, or destroyed. Four thousand Jewish men, women, and children were savagely killed. Thousands more quickly converted to Christianity in order to save their lives.

The king, anxious to keep the peace, ordered a halt to the violence and even punished the archdeacon. The mobs, however, only grew angrier. Most high Church leaders and the nobility disliked the violence, which took power from their own hands and placed it in the hands of unstable rabble. In the end, even they were powerless to stop the hate-filled mobs.

Quickly, the violence spread through Castile and Aragon. The once-prosperous Jewish communities of Seville, Cordova, and Toledo were almost totally destroyed. Once-magnificent synagogues were sacked or transformed into churches. In Cordova, the synagogue became the Church of St. Crispin. Today's beautiful Santa Maria la Blanca Church in Toledo was once the city's Great Synagogue.

Some thought the Jewish "problem" would be instantly solved if all Jews accepted Christianity. Following yet another Catholic clergyman, Vincente Ferrer, excited mobs entered synagogues and Jewish quarters to offer Jews a cruel choice: convert or die. Many Jews, not so easily swayed from their ancient religion, either fled their homes or were killed. Thousands of others, scared for their very lives, quickly accepted baptism and suddenly found themselves Christians. One estimate of the number thus converted is thirty-five thousand.

Once converted, whether voluntarily or by force, there was no turning back; the Church considered anyone baptized to be a Christian forever. Even New Christians who managed to flee the country after conversion were, when found, still subject to Church law.

The converts could be divided into three groups. The first was composed of a very small number of Jews who enthusiastically discarded their Jewish culture and began to lead totally Christian lives. A few were even rabbis and scholars. One, Jeshua Halorqi, changed his name to Geronimo de Santa Fe and traveled through Spain converting other Jews. He wrote against the beliefs of his former religion and even made up lies about the Talmud to further his arguments.

A second group was made up of Jews, many wealthy and powerful, who, although converts, quietly honored their Jewish roots. Some encouraged their children to marry into the families of Spanish nobility. Many a poor Christian noble was delighted to marry the rich daughter of a former Jew. Within a generation these children lost whatever attachment their parents once had to their old faith.

Most of the converts, however, were far from sincere in their new faith and kept Jewish tradition alive for themselves and their children. Those who had not been very observant as Jews now continued as unobservant Christians. Most of the converts, however, retained a strong sense of Jewish identity. They had, after all, converted to Christianity only to save their lives.

Outwardly the New Christians were no different from the Old Christians. Their children were baptized and married in church. They supported Christian charities and attended religious services regularly.

Within the privacy of their own families, however, they continued to practice Judaism as well as they could. Secretly, they attended synagogue services. When a child was baptized, the parents symbolically wiped the holy water off the infant as soon as the family returned home from church. Most married among themselves and although the public ceremony took place in a church, a secret Jewish service followed.

New Christians were welcomed into Spanish society with great rejoicing. As Jews, they had been kept out of important professions, government posts, and the army. Now, almost overnight, they found that as Christians, no position was unreachable. Some even became priests and monks. In just a few years both Old and New Christians would realize how false and insincere this artificial religious equality was.

With all the attention paid to the new converts, Jews who did not convert but remained true to their faith were at first ignored by the clergy and the mobs, but not for long. In the continuing attempt to convince Jews to convert, a new tool was discovered—the disputation. Disputations were formal public debates on religious subjects between Jewish and Christian scholars. If the Jews would only listen, the Christians reasoned, they would quickly discover the error of their ways and accept Christianity.

The most famous disputation took place, on and off, between February 1413 and November 1414 at Tortosa. Under the sponsorship of Pope Benedict XIII, Catholic scholars, including the turncoat Geronimo de Santa Fe, posed the following question for debate: Has the Messiah, in the person of Jesus Christ, already appeared, and did the Talmud actually accept him?

Arguing persuasively on the Jewish side was an equally distinguished group led by Vidal Benviniste. Although the Jewish scholars presented the best defense possible, they always had to be careful not to offend the Catholic audience.

When the Tortosa Disputation did not produce the expected result of a mass Jewish conversion, in 1414 the pope issued a far-reaching set of regulations against Jews. Henceforth, Jews were forbidden to study the Talmud or build new synagogues; each community, no matter what its size, could have only one Jewish house of worship. Trades and professions previously open to Jews were severely restricted; Jews could no longer be physicians or pharmacists, for example. All had to wear the distinctive yellow badge on their clothing. They were not allowed to bake or distribute matzoh, the unleavened bread eaten on Passover. And to further the humiliation, all Jews over the age of twelve were required to listen to a Christian sermon three times a year, often directly from a synagogue pulpit.

During those years some Jews continued to accept Christianity, by force or by choice. However, the mass conversions expected by the preachers did not happen. Instead, those Christians who earlier rejoiced over the conversions began to have second thoughts, for the New Christians not only continued the business lives they had led as Jews, but now successfully entered all aspects of Spanish society that had previously been closed to them.

As the New Christians maintained close relations with their Jewish friends and neighbors, the Spanish Church grew increasingly concerned about these converts who were legally Christians but inwardly Jewish. In fact, the hatred of the masses for the New Christians, or Marranos, was even greater than against Jews who had not converted. In 1467 a particularly bloody uprising took place in Toledo with heavy casualties among the Marranos. In 1473 similar attacks took place in Cordova. There, during a religious procession, a young Marrano girl accidentally spilled dirty water out a window, which splashed on an image of the Virgin Mary. The crowd, urged on by fanatics, instantly set upon the Marranos. Even when the local nobility tried to intervene and restore order, the unruly mobs would not listen.

The violence continued for three days and spread to other cities. Eventually, concern about the true devotion of the Marranos to Christianity and jealousy over their successes led to demands for the establishment of a religious court, or Inquisition, to investigate those not totally loyal to the Church. Soon the spirit of the Inquisition would invade every town, home, and heart in Spain.

FOUR

Baptism by Fire

"Here envious hate and slanderous tongues have made me pass my life."

FRIAR LUIS DE LEON,
AN INQUISITION PRISONER

The concept of the Inquisition was not new. The Church had used courts of this sort before in its history to search out those who were not "good" Catholics. Despite the prevalent anti-Jewish feelings among the populace, the Inquisition was permitted to deal only with Catholics who had strayed from the Church.

Laws were now passed preventing New Christians from holding certain appointed positions in government or the Church. Violence against them increased. In 1467 a bloody war broke out in Toledo between Marranos and Old Christians. In 1468 the bishop of Cordova founded an anti-Marrano fraternity called the Christian Brotherhood. No matter how Christian the Marranos had become, to the Old Christians their Jewish bloodline still made them impure.

In 1469 Ferdinand II, heir to the throne of the kingdom of

27

Aragon, married Isabella, the eighteen-year-old princess of Castile. Both Jews and New Christians wished to see a strong central government to counteract the power of the nobles and the Church. In fact, the two men who were instrumental in arranging the royal marriage were a Jew and a Marrano, Don Abraham Senior and Alfonso de Quintanilla. Both would live to regret their deed.

Isabella was wealthy; her suitor, Ferdinand, was poor. Senior raised money among the Jews to provide Ferdinand with a loan. Quintanilla presented the beautiful bride with an expensive necklace in the name of the groom.

Ferdinand had known Jews at his father's court, and although he tried to hide the fact, his great-grandmother was a Jewish lady from Toledo. Isabella had grown up in a Catholic convent, away from the everyday world. While their backgrounds differed, both at first welcomed Jewish financial assistance in waging war against the Moslems.

Gradually, however, the monarchs were swayed by the anti-Jewish position of the clergy and nobility. The growing cries for an Inquisition appealed to both monarchs, though perhaps for different reasons. The devout Isabella welcomed the expulsion of unbelieving Marranos, which would strengthen the Church. From a political standpoint it was wise for the monarchs to support the wishes of the clergy and the nobles for an Inquisition. Moreover, Ferdinand saw that the riches of the Marranos would fall into his treasury.

In 1478 the pope issued his approval for the establishment of an official Inquisition Tribunal in Spain. Two years later, King Ferdinand and Queen Isabella appointed the first inquisitors and the serious work of ferreting out disloyal Christians was under way. The Inquisition would legally continue in Spain until the early nineteenth century.

Baptism by Fire

The people of Seville greeted the establishment of the Inquisition with great joy, but the Marranos and many of the nobility tried to prevent the tribunal from operating in their city. They knew that the rules under which the Inquisition operated were unfair.

Yet, as the inquisitors entered Seville for the first time, they were grandly received in a splendid official procession. With the ceremonies over, it was time for the tribunal members to begin their "holy" work. Their job was to search out and punish Judaizers—those who showed even the slightest sign of supporting or observing a Jewish law, custom, or tradition. The Inquisitors began by setting a trap. They invited any guilty Marrano to come forward and confess with no fear of punishment. Once those unfortunates presented themselves they received a surprise demand: Provide the Inquisition with the names of friends and relatives who might also be Judaizers or go to jail. From that moment on there was no lack of victims for the Inquisition.

Judaizing was a difficult crime to detect. The inquisitors had a law passed which listed over thirty ways to recognize the guilty. Here are a few of the "telltale" signs:

1. Celebrating the Sabbath by wearing a clean shirt, not lighting a fire, or not working.
2. Eating meat during Lent, a Christian period of fasting.
3. Not eating or drinking on the Jewish Day of Atonement.
4. Washing hands before praying.
5. Blessing a cup of wine before eating.
6. Not eating pork.
7. Giving Old Testament names to children.

"La Sentence," a depiction of the accused receiving the verdict of the Inquisition. *Courtesy New York Public Library Picture Collection.*

Not only Marranos but many practicing Christians were accused, simply for doing something that appeared "Jewish" in nature. One woman was turned over to the Inquisition when she set a white cloth on her dinner table on a Friday evening. Jealous relatives informed on each other, disgruntled servants on their masters, students on their teachers: sometimes acting out of conscience and sometimes out of revenge.

Official Inquisition spies, called confidants, were everywhere. They sneaked through the narrow streets of Marrano neighborhoods and peeked into windows. They listened to shop gossip and questioned servants. They were particularly active on Friday evenings and on Saturdays, the Jewish Sabbath.

Although punishment given out by the Inquisition varied, two common practices were confiscation of property and burning at the stake. The guilty had all property taken from them and their families. Once-wealthy Marrano families suddenly were penniless as the treasuries of the Church and the crown grew immense. Even people long dead were brought to trial in absentia. When their graves were found, they were opened and the remains burned. The wealth willed to children and grandchildren was confiscated and the family bloodline was no longer considered "pure."

Bishop Arias of Avila, although a high Church official, was the grandson of Jews. Seeking to erase any trace of his background, he secretly stole into the Jewish cemetery at night, dug up his grandparents' bones, and burned them. Had the Inquisition done the burning, the bishop's future would have been greatly endangered. In that atmosphere of fear even bishops with Jewish backgrounds could not escape accusation.

Likewise, anyone fortunate enough to escape from the clutches of the Inquisition could be burned in effigy. A doll representing the accused was thrown into the fire. That symbolic act allowed the authorities to confiscate whatever property that person had left behind.

Death by burning was conducted in a public ceremony known as the auto-da-fé, or Act of Faith. Its drama and ritual were designed to impress the populace. Because the Church did not wish to actually shed blood, the condemned were turned over to the civil authorities to carry out the death order.

The first auto-da-fé in Seville took place on February 6, 1481, when six people were burned at the stake in front of a large crowd of nobles, clergy, and citizens. Month after month, year after year, the sight of the auto-da-fe became a common occurrence as the Inquisition spread throughout Spain.

By coincidence, 1481 marked the beginning of a terrible plague that lasted through 1488. In Seville alone, fifteen thousand people died. The disease did not discriminate among Jew, Marrano, or Catholic. Some saw the plague as a punishment.

Within a short time it was clear that the business of running an Inquisition was more complicated than originally imagined. To provide a central leadership, a national council of all the local tribunals was created. Tomás de Torquemada was appointed Inquisitor-General of Spain on October 17, 1483. Ironically, it was rumored that Torquemada himself had Jewish ancestors!

The sixty-three-year-old priest set out to organize and refine the process of searching out and punishing the heretics. He established a constitution that legalized the inquisitors' practices and ordered tribunals founded in cities throughout the country. Soon, the operations of the Inquisition became a second government in Spain. The king and the nobility were powerless to stop its work.

A network of prisons was set up. Informers everywhere were ready to turn in a neighbor, business rival, or even a relative, whether guilty or not. Sometimes a prisoner had a short wait for a trial; sometimes not. The outcome was almost never in doubt. Very few went free.

Torture was refined as a tool for extracting confessions. Water torture, the thumbscrew, and the rack were used to extract confessions from the innocent as well as from the guilty. Even if a prisoner had done nothing wrong, weeks and months of painful torture often resulted in a "confession."

This typical outdoor scene shows the diverse phases of the auto-da-fé. *Courtesy Museo del Prado, Madrid.*

The Spanish Inquisition required the condemned to wear a cone-shaped hat and a special shirt called a *sanbenito*. *Courtesy New York Public Library Picture Collection.*

The speed with which a person confessed usually affected the sentence. Punishment ranged from fines, confiscation of property, life imprisonment, to burning at the stake. Even the death by fire had a "nice" touch. If the condemned asked for the mercy of the Church, he was strangled to death before his body was burned. Those who continued to defy the Church were burned alive.

The auto-da-fé was a wickedly impressive ceremony to watch. It was held in a prominent plaza and staged like a theatrical presentation. Dignitaries, dressed in colorful official uniforms, were prominently seated. Church officials wore their finest vestments. When all was in readiness a procession formed. At its head flew the large banner of the Inquisition. Behind it marched the Inquisition officials. Next came the prisoners, dressed in unique costumes. They wore *sanbenitos,* or large vests, upon which were drawn designs and phrases indicating the crime: "This person has Judaized!" A cone-shaped hat sat on their heads. The prisoners were barefoot and each carried a tall yellow candle.

After the verdict of the tribunal was read, the procession regrouped. Those sentenced to death were turned over to the civil authorities for execution, which took place as soon as the auto-da-fé was over. According to one historical source, the Spanish Inquisition dealt with over three hundred thousand cases and sentenced at least thirty thousand to death.

FIVE

Expulsion

"Oh Majesty, save your loyal subjects. Why do you
act so cruelly toward us?"

DON ISAAC ABRAVANEL
TO KING FERDINAND, 1492

A s we have seen, most of the Jews of Spain had been living
under severe restrictions since 1371. They wore the humiliat-
ing yellow badge to single them out in public and could not have
any dealings, business or personal, with Christians.

Restricted to the Juderias, the Jews were allowed to engage in
limited occupations only. Some were tailors, jewelers, traders, book-
binders, and silversmiths. A few rich men were moneylenders or tax
farmers, appointed by the king to collect taxes from a specific population group.

Taxes were heavy. The Jews were taxed not only by the king—
perhaps the reason they were so "protected"—but by the archbishops
of the Church as well. On top of these official taxes, they also paid a

tax on meat and wine to their local Jewish government to support community religious and educational institutions.

The hard life took its toll on Jews. The level of Jewish scholarship in Spain after 1371 dropped dramatically. The number of distinguished rabbis and scholars declined sharply. During that period, large numbers of Jewish children grew up with little or no religious education and many adults could not even read enough Hebrew to participate in traditional services.

With all the upheaval in the life of the Jewish community, something had to be done to restore self-respect. In 1432, the chief rabbi, Abraham Benveniste, opened a conference of the country's leading rabbis and leaders. Their goal was to establish a set of rules for the government of the Jewish community. Deeply concerned by the decreasing interest in education, they agreed to develop and fund religious schools for all Jewish children and adopted regulations governing religious services.

One unique problem addressed by the conference was clothing. Like other people, Jews enjoyed wearing fine clothes and jewelry in public. Non-Jews found it disgraceful that members of the "hated race" should dress like them. The conference voted that Jews should be cautious about wearing expensive clothes so as not to offend Christians. The once proud and vital Jewish communities of Spain had grown timid and weak—with good reason.

The second half of the fifteenth century brought changes in the conditions of both Marranos and Jews. For the Jews, life improved somewhat under the reigns of Henry IV of Castile (1454–1474) and John II of Aragon (1456–1479), the predecessors of Ferdinand and Isabella. The stricter anti-Jewish laws were ignored and some Jews were even appointed to public office. Many Jews took advantage of this relaxed climate and moved from the Juderias of the large cities to smaller towns throughout Spain.

In 1480 Ferdinand and Isabella ordered all Jews to again live in separate quarters of Spanish cities. In 1483 the monarchs expelled Jews from the southern province of Andalusia, including the cities of Seville and Cordova. The intention was to remove totally any contact between Jews and Marranos in that populous area. The Jews of Spain could not foresee that nine years later they would be expelled from the entire country.

Perhaps one fact that comforted the Jews was that Ferdinand and Isabella surrounded themselves with Jewish and Marrano officials in high positions. Don Abraham Senior, the man who made their marriage possible, was named chief rabbi by the monarchs. Luis de Santangel was a trusted adviser.

Perhaps the most interesting Jewish personality at the court was Don Isaac Abravanel. Abravanel was descended from an old Spanish-Jewish family who a century earlier had fled the country for Portugal to escape the 1391 massacres. There they established themselves in business. Abravanel's father eventually became financial adviser to the king of Portugal, a position inherited by Don Isaac. It was at the court that Don Isaac met a Genoese sailor, Christopher Columbus. Within a few years both men would meet again at another court and together change the course of world history.

In the 1490s, Portugal was engaged in a costly and losing war with Spanish Castile. As minister of finance, Don Isaac Abravanel was blamed for the failures. In 1483, King Joao of Portugal, intending to punish those he thought responsible for the war's failure, planned to arrest Don Isaac. When he heard about the king's plan in advance, Abravanel, accompanied by his son-in-law, hastily fled over the border to safety in Spain. King Joao promptly confiscated all of Abravanel's property in Portugal.

Don Isaac, now nearly penniless, settled in Toledo to a quiet life of scholarship and writing. His authoritative commentaries on the Bible are still in use today. But his reputation had preceded him and in March 1484 he was summoned to an audience at the royal palace. The king and queen of Spain were suitably impressed and invited him to become financial agent to the court. He gradually rebuilt much of his own wealth and became a reliable source of loans to the king and queen. In 1491 he became Queen Isabella's personal financial agent.

As the Inquisition intensified its work, Don Isaac's presence at the court provided Spanish Jews with a false sense of security. After all, they reasoned, the monarchs would not seriously harm them while the court was so dependent on Jews for financial support.

In the years just before the Expulsion of 1492, Jews needed all the security they could find. Not content with chasing down and burning Marranos, Torquemada and Church leaders kept trying to humiliate and discredit Jews by depicting them as inhuman. The average Spaniard living in such a society believed any evil rumor about Jews. The most widespread one was the blood libel. Jews, it was falsely but commonly repeated, needed the blood of young Christian children in their rituals.

But in order to make a strong case for expulsion, Torquemada had to show "proof" of an alleged crime. The perfect situation arose when one Benito Garcia was arrested and found guilty of being a Judaizing Marrano.

In the course of torture he readily confessed to the inquisitors that he had been taught Judaism by a Jewish father and son, Ca Franco and Yuce Franco. In the spirit of the Inquisition, the hapless Francos were immediately thrown into jail. When the elder Franco took ill and requested a rabbi's visit, the inquisitors saw a wonderful opportunity. A rabbi came to Franco's cell and comforted the old man. In the course of their conversation, the rabbi began talking about ritual murders. Franco did not then understand why.

In truth, the "rabbi" was a priest. True, he had formerly been a Jew and a real rabbi, but now he was a New Christian and a Catholic priest, Father Cuviquez. Standing behind the door to Franco's cell during this visit was the prison doctor. Later, under solemn oath, the doctor would testify in full truth that he overheard ritual murder being discussed. Later, after continuous torture, the younger Franco "admitted" his own guilt in the murder of a Christian boy. The rabbis had given him the idea, he said.

This was the moment Tomás de Torquemada was waiting for. With full publicity, the grand inquisitor himself entered the case and news of this "proof" of Jewish ritual murder of Christian children spread throughout the land. People throughout the country demanded the removal of the "Jewish menace" from Spain.

King Ferdinand congratulated Torquemada on his unmasking of the "evil" Jews. For the king and queen this was the perfect excuse to expel the Jews from Spain.

With the fall of Granada on January 2, 1492, the monarchs found themselves heavily in debt to Jewish creditors. The royal treasury was empty. Cloaking himself in holiness, the king saw a way out of his financial trouble. On March 31, 1492, in the beautiful Alhambra Palace in Granada, just captured from the Moors, he signed a decree ordering all Spanish Jews to convert to Christianity within four months or leave the country. The Jews stood accused of aiding the Marranos and swaying them from their new religion. The very presence of Jews, the edict explained, gave Marranos access to kosher food, prayer books, and matzohs for Passover.

Rather than convert, most Jews chose to leave the only country they had ever known. The king's decree forbade them from taking along any gold or silver: they left with only their religion and their beloved Spanish language and culture.

As Don Isaac Abravanel pleaded with Ferdinand and Isabella to change their minds, the ever-vigilant Torquemada lurked in the shadows. There was no turning back.

It is estimated that more than two hundred thousand Jews fled Spain by August 2, 1492, the last possible day set by royal decree. Each Jewish family that left Spain had its own tale of personal tragedy. Even Don Isaac Abravanel, once so high in royal circles, was not spared, since he refused to convert to Christianity. In an attempt to prevent the brilliant financial adviser from leaving the country, King Ferdinand ordered the kidnapping of Don Isaac's grandson. Surely, the king reasoned, the old man would then convert to remain behind with his beloved grandson. Don Isaac and his son, Judah, learned of the plan in advance and hastily sent the boy to safety in Portugal. Unfortunately, Portugal was soon closed to Jewish travel, and the boy was never again seen by his family.

In contrast, after much soul searching, Abraham Senior, the man who helped unite Ferdinand and Isabella in marriage, accepted baptism at age eighty and remained at the court.

The months leading up to the day of expulsion were filled with grief and anguish as Jews who had lived in Spain for generations realized that their lives here were over. Anguish and despair prevailed.

But no one had time to sit and ponder fate. First, they needed to sell all their property—the homes, farms, businesses, and furniture accumulated over the years. Nothing of value could be taken out of the country. But with so many departing, the amount of property for sale forced prices to ridiculously low levels. Some des-

perate Jews sold an orchard for a broken-down mule or a valuable
house for a rickety cart; the immediate goal for many was to reach a
Spanish port and find a sea passage to safety.

They made arrangements with their Christian neighbors to
maintain the cemeteries being left behind. Their beautiful synagogues would be quickly transformed into churches, convents, or
even stables.

To meet the expulsion deadline, many Jews fled Spain in overcrowded
ships. *Courtesy Beth Hatefutsoth, The Nahum Goldmann Museum of the
Jewish Diaspora, Israel.*

The roads were crowded with these unfortunates carrying with them the pitiful remains of their former lives. As the Jews made their way toward those ports, they were led by musicians trying to make the misery more bearable. Rabbis passed among them to offer comfort and reassurance.

Christians who observed the heart-wrenching scenes could offer only one piece of advice: Convert while you still can and remain in the land of your birth. While some Jews did reluctantly accept baptism in order to remain, most did not. Even to the moment of boarding ship many hoped that a last-minute miracle would rescue them.

Those seeking passage out of the country were often at the mercy of cruel ship captains as well as the normal dangers of the sea. Of twenty-five ships that sailed from Cadiz and St. Mary to North Africa, seventeen sank during a fearsome storm at sea. When the remaining ships put in to the port of Malaga for emergency refitting and supplies, four hundred Jewish families on board lost heart and sadly accepted baptism just to remain on Spanish soil. The remainder bravely resumed their journey to Fez. Of these hardy souls, many were robbed and murdered on the high seas.

As these horror stories reached the remaining Jews in Spain, still more saw conversion as the only way to save themselves and their families. This time it was their Marrano relatives and friends who offered comfort. Soon they alone would remain as forlorn remnants of a once proud and prosperous Jewish community in Spain. The 1492 Expulsion Edict of Ferdinand and Isabella was officially withdrawn only on December 16, 1968.

Those who survived the long journey from their Spanish homes ultimately settled and reestablished their lives in far-off cities in France, Italy, North Africa, Holland, and Turkey. Don Isaac Abra-

A representation of the Jewish expulsion from Spain and Portugal.
Courtesy Beth Hatefutsoth, The Nahum Goldmann Museum of the Jewish Diaspora, Israel.

vanel, after much wandering, found a new home in Naples. He was in financial ruin but settled down to a life of scholarship and writing. It was not long before his presence became known to the local ruler and Abravanel again assumed a respected position in yet another royal court.

The Jews who left Spain were called Sephardim, after the Hebrew name for Spain. Other Jews in Europe at the time of the Expulsion were called Ashkenazim, or Jews of German and East European heritage. Always more numerous than their Sephardic brethren, the Ashkenazic Jews experienced their own share of expulsions and discrimination. Yet, unlike their Sephardic brethren, they largely lived apart from fellow countrymen and concerned themselves only with Jewish life.

What made the Expulsion from Spain so devastating was that Spanish culture, tradition, and civilization were so much a part of the lives of the Sephardim. They carried this heritage with them into exile.

From this time on, only the former Jewish streets in Seville, Toledo, and other cities remained as evidence that a vibrant, colorful, and active Jewish civilization once existed in Spain.

Meanwhile, heading out to sea away from Europe, Columbus was on his way to a New World. Jews and Marranos had made it possible for him to sail; soon their troubled descendants would gratefully benefit from his discovery.

SIX

The Trail of Hidden Tears

"Esther did not reveal her people or her kindred."

BOOK OF ESTHER 2:10

Spain shares a long common border with Portugal. Together these countries make up the Iberian Peninsula. It made sense, then, for Jews to seek a haven in Portugal.

King Joao II, as head of a Catholic country, at first decided to prevent Jews from crossing his border. However, after delicate negotiations he agreed to let thirty important Jewish families, including that of Isaac Aboab, the chief rabbi of Spain, settle in the Portuguese city of Oporto. Other Jews, upon payment of 100 cruzados for each adult, were also allowed to settle in the country. For less wealthy Jews the payment of eight cruzados per adult allowed a temporary haven in Portugal not to exceed eight months. It is thought that nearly a hundred thousand Spanish Jews grasped at this opportunity.

The king promised to find ship's passage for Jews going to other countries, but the number of ships made available for this venture was woefully inadequate. When the eight months were up, those Jews who were temporary residents were declared slaves and sold. Hundreds of Jewish children were forcibly taken from their parents and sent to populate the inhospitable island of Saint Thomas off the coast of Africa. Nearly all soon died.

When Joao II died, he was succeeded by Manoel, a young cousin who sought the hand of Ferdinand and Isabella's daughter in marriage. But the Spanish monarchs would not approve of the marriage until King Manoel had rid his kingdom of the Jews who had fled there from Spain.

Manoel did not want to jeopardize his chance to marry the distinguished young Spanish princess. At the same time he did not want to lose the industrious Jews. He came upon a cruelly simple decision. In March 1497 he ordered all Jewish children between the ages of four and fourteen to be taken from their parents and baptized. He thought the parents would follow their children into Christianity. Those who would not convert would have to leave the country.

The Jews were grief stricken. Some killed their own children rather than see them baptized. Others committed suicide. Not many Jews accepted conversion. To add to the horror, some zealous Portuguese officials forcibly dragged unwilling Jews into churches and baptized them or sprinkled holy water on them from a distance. Once they were baptized, whether willingly or by force, those Jews were considered Christians.

Nearly twenty thousand Jews were gathered in Lisbon to await deportation. While they waited in hunger and misery, Portuguese officials urged them to reconsider and accept baptism. The Jews were kept waiting past the legal date of departure and then were declared slaves because they were still in the country. Gradually many yielded to the continual pressure and converted. Some who were able to escape found safety in Italy, Greece, Africa, or Turkey.

In the end there was no expulsion as there had been in Spain. Instead, the Jews of Portugal were forcibly converted, although they practiced their Jewish faith secretly as best they could and passed their traditions down to their children. Officially, after 1492 in Spain and 1497 in Portugal, no Jews lived anywhere on the Iberian Peninsula. The Old Christians, however, continued to harbor distrust and hatred of the New Christians. Marrano families continually sought any opportunity to flee Portugal. So many escaped that in 1499 the king established a law prohibiting New Christians from leaving the country.

For his part, the Portuguese king attempted to stop the flow of his best business people by promising that the Marranos would be left alone for twenty years; no criminal charges would be brought against them on religious grounds. At the end of that period they would be answerable only to regular courts: no Inquisition would be established. This temporary interlude gave the secret Jews time to establish firmly a limited form of Jewish religious practice among themselves.

As "official" as the Marranos now were, they still could not escape the anti-Jewish emotions around them. They were victims of periodic attacks until in 1507 King Manoel lifted the ban on emigration. Many took advantage of this opportunity and for the next several years Marranos freely left Portugal for other countries where their relatives and friends had previously settled. There, once out of reach of Portuguese authorities, they returned to Judaism. In 1521 this freedom to emigrate was halted when the king realized just how many Marranos, and how much of their wealth, had left his kingdom. Life in Lisbon became even more dangerous for the Marranos.

From this point, the Marranos remaining in Portugal had to seek out secret routes to safety. Many requested permission to travel on business to other Christian countries. The ports of Italy and the Low Countries (the Netherlands and Belgium) were favorites since a higher level of religious tolerance existed there than in Portugal. Secret Marrano groups were established in major cities of Europe to help newcomers and advise them on living conditions. Some Marranos joined Jews already established in such cities as Antwerp, Ancona, or Ferrara. Others trekked through treacherous mountain passes or endured dangerous sea voyages to reach safe haven in Turkey or North Africa.

It did not take long for the authorities to realize that the seemingly innocent business trips were really excuses for escape. By 1532 the Low Countries of Europe were closed to all New Christian travelers.

In 1525, when the new king, Joao III, following in the footsteps of a preceding monarch, decided to marry a Spanish princess—this time the granddaughter of Ferdinand and Isabella—talk of an Inquisition in Portugal began anew. After numerous delays won by the Marranos, and despite earlier promises, the Inquisition was formally instituted in Portugal in 1539. Its establishment was due in large measure to an incident that occurred in Lisbon.

On a February morning, people noticed large signs nailed to church doors: THE MESSIAH HAS NOT COME. JESUS IS NOT THE REAL MESSIAH. Although a Marrano, accused of the act, was tortured and burned to death, the people's anger was not satisfied. On September 20, 1540, the first formal auto-da-fé took place on Portuguese soil. The burnings continued, off and on, until 1765.

In that climate of suspicion it was almost impossible to observe any Jewish practices. Yet the Marranos managed to develop a very limited version of Jewish ritual. They substituted Portuguese for Hebrew in religious services and dropped those obvious practices that could mark them as Jews. Although the language limitation put many Jewish texts, including the Talmud, out of reach, the Bible, in translation, became the main guide to their faith.

So as not to call undue attention to themselves, the Marranos incorporated certain traditional Christian practices into their ritual. They did not cover their heads during services and knelt when praying. While pork was now on their menus, they tried to avoid eating it on Jewish holidays. They continued to light Sabbath candles, but only in the utmost secrecy in a windowless cellar or inside an earthenware jar. Their church attendance was not regular, but frequent enough so their neighbors would notice their presence.

Since Christians could know when it was time for a Jewish religious holiday, the Marranos made it a practice to observe major holidays a day or two earlier or later than usual. They especially

This 1480 prayer book for Yom Kippur, the Day of Atonement, is shaped in such a way that it can be slipped up a sleeve and hidden by the Marrano using it. *Courtesy Jewish Theological Seminary Library, New York.*

observed Yom Kippur, the Day of Atonement, and Passover, the holiday marking the Jewish release from Egyptian slavery.

They also found comfort and inspiration in Purim, the holiday that commemorates Queen Esther, the Jewish maiden who hid her religious background and was able to save her people from death. Each Purim they read in the Book of Esther, "Esther did not reveal her people or her kindred."

Like the earlier Marranos of Spain, they found it dangerous to instruct children about their real faith. It was only when a child reached adolescence that the "secret" was revealed. As each generation passed on, less and less of authentic Jewish learning and tradition remained. In time, many Marranos simply became part of the greater Christian society, but a sizeable number over the generations continued to secretly practice their limited Judaism.

Over the years, many more Marranos were able to leave Portugal and rejoin their ancient religion. Within one hundred and fifty years after the Expulsion from Spain, Jews and Marranos were spread across the globe. Sizeable communities existed in such far-off places as North Africa, Italy, France, Germany, Turkey, and later the New World. Although some of these destinations were Christian, the Marranos at least found themselves removed from the direct harsh and dangerous atmosphere of the Inquisition.

During that period rabbis continually ruled that Marranos had a legitimate place within the Jewish community according to Jewish law. Their rulings reflected the friendly and sympathetic acceptance shown the Marranos by most Jews.

Wherever they went the refugees carried with them the memories of Spain. Their names were Spanish or Portuguese; they spoke Ladino, a language of Spanish origin still in use by their descendants today. In some communities synagogues bore the names of towns in

Spain, which their ancestors had left in 1492. In this century, a historian visiting with a Jewish family of Spanish heritage in Bulgaria was surprised when the man showed him a rusty key. "It is that of our house in Toledo which perhaps still stands," he wistfully explained.

The scattering of Jews and Marranos did not take place overnight, nor did the refugees find immediate acceptance in their new homes. In Naples, the first large group of exiles from Spain in 1492 was accused of bringing a terrible plague to the city.

Ferdinand, the kindly king of Naples, intervened and protected the Jews, who had already survived a danger-filled journey. But protection was not guaranteed. Don Isaac Abravanel, after serving as adviser to the king of Naples, was himself forced to flee to Sicily when Naples was captured by the French. He traveled from Sicily to Corfu and, in 1503, to Venice, where again his diplomatic services were requested by the city's senate.

Venice was a popular destination for many Marranos. Although officially banned from the city in 1497, they gained entrance as Christians: many continued on to Turkey. Beginning in 1516, Venice's sizeable Jewish community was restricted to the Ghetto, apart from the Christian population. Even so, on arrival in Venice some Marranos publicly shed their Christian pasts and settled in the Ghetto as practicing Jews.

Other Italian cities offering refuge were Ferrara and Ancona. In both ports, Jewish businesses thrived as trade blossomed with other countries. The dispersion of Jews and Marranos created a ready-made international business network.

Jewish refugees from Spain arrived in Ferrara in 1492. Forty-five years later, Marranos escaping from Portugal were welcomed by the earlier Jewish settlers. Unlike Jews who arrived earlier, the new-

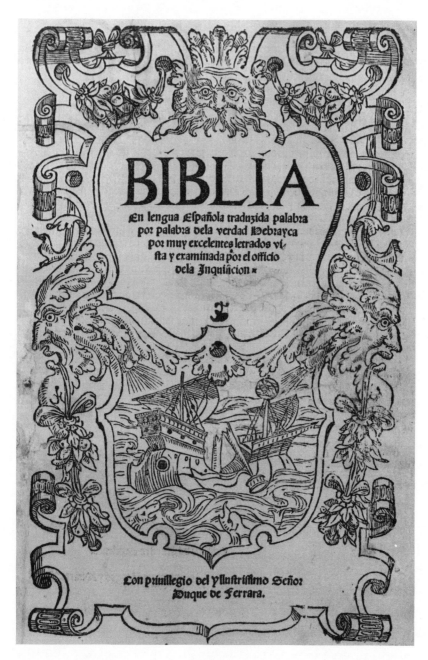

Title page of the Ferrara Bible, 1553, which was translated into Spanish for use by Marranos. *Courtesy Jewish Theological Seminary Library, New York.*

comers were far removed from Jewish learning and tradition. To help them learn about their heritage, books on Jewish learning were printed in Spanish. Ferrara soon became a center of Jewish publishing. The first Spanish translation of the Prayer Book was printed there in 1552, followed a few years later by the Ferrara Bible. Lest they forget that they were still living in a Catholic land, Jews opening the Ferrara Bible found a notice printed on the title page indicating that the work had been examined by the Office of the Inquisition.

The Ferrara Bible was dedicated to the most famous Jewish woman of the sixteenth century, Dona Gracia Nasi. Born into a Portuguese Marrano family, Dona Gracia married a wealthy merchant and banker, Francisco Mendes. Upon the death of her husband in 1536, with a newly established Inquisition creating life-and-death problems for Marranos, Dona Gracia and her family sought an escape route with the ultimate goal of returning to Judaism. Her wealth and family connections made it possible for her to travel and live in a number of European cities. Gradually, she transferred much of her European wealth to Turkey and settled there in 1553. She was a charitable person who furthered Jewish causes with her intellect and money.

Bajazet II, the sultan of Turkey, was overjoyed with the arrival of the Marranos. With Christian Europe largely closed to them, the newcomers brought their knowledge of business and finance to Turkey. From this base of commercial power, the Marranos—returned now to their Jewish faith—became wealthy and respected international traders. They did not, however, forget their Spanish and Portuguese origins; they spoke Spanish and surrounded themselves with Spanish culture. New arrivals from the clutches of the Inquisition brought the latest news from home. By the middle of the 1500s over

Rembrandt's *The Jewish Bride*. The painter lived in Amsterdam's Jewish quarter and often used its residents as subjects of his paintings. *Courtesy Rijksmuseum, Holland.*

fifteen thousand Jews were living in Constantinople, the Turkish capital.

They used their power and wealth to help their brethren in Christian Europe. When a formal Inquisition was established in Ancona, Italy, the Jews of Turkey were outraged, and when twenty-four Marranos of Ancona were burned in an auto-da-fé in 1556, the Jews of Turkey banded together to seek revenge.

Under the leadership of Dona Gracia Nasi, a meeting was held in Constantinople at which an economic boycott of the port of Ancona was announced. The sultan of Turkey, in support of his Jewish subjects, even sent an ambassador to Ancona to demand the release of Marranos held in the prisons of the Inquisition. Although the boycott was not a total success, it marked the first time in modern history that Jews had the strength and will to use their economic and political power to seek justice for themselves.

Marranos did not arrive in Holland until 1593. When King Philip II of Spain, who had earlier gained control over the Netherlands, was deposed, Marrano families set sail for the relative freedom of Holland. At first, the Marranos kept their Judaism secret—Amsterdam was as yet an unsafe place—but many settled there and contributed greatly to the prosperity of the port.

Their connections with Marranos in other countries and their knowledge of languages helped them make Amsterdam a world center for trade and shipping. Many became wealthy and figured prominently in the life of the city. In time, encouraged by the city's tolerant attitudes, many openly returned to Judaism.

The Marrano advance in Holland and other European countries was helped by religious upheaval in the Christian world. As Protestant churches came into existence as a result of Martin Luther's Reformation, begun in 1517, there was a greater tolerance for religious differences, particularly in northern Europe.

The Jews of Spain were not the only Jews ever expelled from European homes. Stories of expulsions fill Jewish history: England in 1290, France in 1394, Frankfurt in 1614. One result of these expulsions was the movement of Ashkenazic Jews eastward across Europe into the backwoods of Poland and Russia. There they led rural and unsophisticated lives exclusively centered on Jewish religion, study, and society. Unlike the Sephardim, the Jews of eastern Europe conducted their lives apart from their non-Jewish neighbors.

The Sephardic Jews, on the other hand, mainly dispersed from cosmopolitan Spain and Portugal to similar lands of relative opportunity. By 1656, due in part to a petition by the Dutch rabbi Manasseh Ben Israel, Jews, expelled in 1290, were once again allowed to live in England. Soon they and the Jews of Holland would greatly contribute to the development of the New World across the ocean.

SEVEN

An Uncertain Refuge

"It is our fervent wish that you treat the Jewish Nation
on a basis of equality with all other residents. . . ."

DIRECTORS OF THE DUTCH WEST INDIA COMPANY
TO THE SUPREME COUNCIL IN RECIFE, 1646

Luis de Torres, Christopher Columbus's Marrano interpreter, was the first European to set foot on the soil of the New World. He also became the first Jew to settle there, on the island we now know as Cuba. When Columbus sailed home to report his discovery, Torres stayed behind to cultivate tobacco. He was the first to recognize the economic significance of the "firebrands" smoked by the natives. Soon tobacco became an important European import.

Despite the fact that no practicing Jews were left in Spain, Columbus's second voyage was financed by Jewish funds that had been confiscated by royal decree before the Expulsion. Columbus died in 1506, just a year after Luis de Santangel, the man who made the first voyage possible.

Columbus's great discovery opened the way to further exploration and conquest in search of riches. Within a few years, Spain took possession of lands in the New World and began to settle them. Spain's colonies were divided into two main areas: "New Spain," which consisted of what is today a good part of the southwestern United States, Mexico, Central America, and the Caribbean islands, and "Peru," which consisted of all South America except Brazil and Panama.

Quickly, Jews and Marranos found their way across the Atlantic to establish new homes. They hoped to find refuge from the Inquisition. In 1493 Spain issued orders forbidding Jews to live anywhere in the Spanish colonies of the New World. Yet as early as 1495 Marrano settlers could be found in Hispaniola (now divided between the Dominican Republic and Haiti). Likewise, records from 1515 show Marranos being sent back to Seville, Spain, from Hispaniola to face trial by the Inquisition.

On April 22, 1500, Brazil was claimed for Portugal by Admiral Pedro Alvarez Cabral. With Cabral was a New Christian, Gaspar de Gama. Another escape route now existed for Jews and Marranos, who secretly made their way to the new colonies. In 1508 the Portuguese also prohibited Jews from settling in the colonies. New Christians, however, were not affected and seized the opportunity to emigrate and form business alliances.

Some Marranos arrived against their will; they were prisoners of the Inquisition who along with other "undesirables" were sentenced to exile in the inhospitable forests of Brazil. Within a short time a sizeable population of secret Jews existed in the New World.

New Christians were among the first businessmen to receive permission to colonize the territories. Unlike the adventurers who set sail from Spain and Portugal in search of gold, treasure, and instant wealth, however, the Marranos came to establish homes and industries far from the Inquisition. Most settled in and near the port of Bahia, Brazil.

The Marranos are credited with the creation of the sugar trade, which was so profitable for Portugal. In the sixteenth century, sugar was very expensive and sold only as medication. Marranos imported sugarcane from Madeira and transplanted it to the rich Brazilian soil. In 1516 the first sugar mill began operating there. By the end of the century there were two hundred sugar mills in the country, most owned and operated by Marranos.

In 1580, Philip II, the king of Spain, gained control of Portugal, thereby widening the activity of the Inquisition. The hunt for Judaizers stretched across the Atlantic. Although an official Inquisition never existed in Brazil, local Church officials had the authority to send suspects back to Lisbon for trial. In Bahia, one Nuno Fernandez was shipped back for reading a banned book and for fasting when his sister died. Anna Alcoforada was caught when she poured out water after the death of a slave, a symbolic Jewish act of mourning.

As the Inquisition took firmer hold in Portugal, many Marranos, whose families had lived in the country for generations, now fled—some to the New World. In 1587 yet another order was issued preventing New Christians from leaving Portugal, but in 1601 the ban was lifted, probably because of the need to populate the colonies.

In 1605, the king—motivated strictly by financial needs—obtained a pardon from the pope for all Marranos under Portuguese authority. Those in Inquisition jails were released and others were forgiven their past crimes. He hoped wealthy Marranos would now choose to remain and enrich the country. The Marranos, however, again took advantage of a temporary leniency and even more left Portugal, some for Brazil.

New Christians were numerous also in the Spanish colonies, particularly in Mexico. The Spaniards were more zealous than the Portuguese and a separate Inquisition was instituted in Mexico in 1571. Three years later the first auto-da-fé in the New World took place there. Perhaps the most prominent victim of the Inquisition in the New World was a Mexican governor, Luis de Carvajal. He was descended from a Jewish family and his wife was a secretly practicing Jew, as was his sister Francesca.

Although the Spanish and the Portuguese were the first to establish colonies in the New World, other European powers soon followed. This was in spite of an official division of the New World between Spain and Portugal in the 1494 Treaty of Tordesillas. England, France, and Holland quickly grasped the importance of these new lands as sources of wealth and power and ignored the treaty.

The Dutch in particular, as members of a Protestant nation who felt no ties to the treaty, were aggressive and adventurous traders. Beginning in 1599 Dutch ships made repeated unauthorized trips to the rich salt deposits on the coast of Venezuela. (Among other reasons, Holland needed immense amounts of salt for its herring industry.)

In 1609 King Philip III of Spain, who had been trying to gain control of the Netherlands, signed a twelve-year truce with Holland. As a result, no conflict between the two powers erupted in Europe, but Dutch merchant ships continually harassed Portuguese ships bound for the New World. The Dutch very much wanted to take control of the rich Portuguese colonies in Brazil.

By the 1620s Amsterdam was one of Europe's most important economic centers. It was also known as a home of religious tolerance. Marranos were made welcome early and the city soon became an important center of Jewish activity. It had become such a welcome home for Jews that many referred to it as the "Dutch Jerusalem."

With so many Marranos returning to their Jewish roots, three synagogues were in operation in Amsterdam by 1624. Two respected rabbis led the over eight hundred Jews in the city. Manasseh ben Israel and Isaac Aboab were both members of Marrano families and had been baptized in their youth.

Relations were maintained with Marranos elsewhere, including Portuguese Brazil. In 1622 the Dutch West India Company was founded in Amsterdam for the purpose of establishing colonies and organizing trading operations in the New World. The Company had the power to appoint governors and officials and otherwise rule any territory conquered from the Portuguese. From the beginning, a number of the Company's board of directors were Jewish businessmen of Amsterdam.

Knowing that Brazil was poorly defended and inhabited by a large Marrano population, the Company organized a military expedition against Bahia, a key Portuguese port. One of the Company's strategies was to rely on the Marrano population for support from within the colony. The New Christians did not disappoint the Dutch. With rumors of a forthcoming Inquisition in Portuguese Brazil, the Marranos gratefully welcomed a Dutch invasion.

On May 8, 1624, residents of Bahia awoke to a frightening sight. Twenty-five heavily armed Dutch ships sat in the harbor, their guns pointing menacingly at the city. The citizens were so terrified and confused that few were able to resist. The three thousand Dutch troops soon overcame the forts guarding the city, and the next day Bahia officially became Dutch.

One of the first declarations by the new Dutch governor granted religious freedom to all residents. No group was happier than the Marranos. Many took advantage of this moment to shed New Christian disguises and announce a return to Judaism. Jews from Holland also began arriving and were greeted warmly by the Marranos.

This era of freedom did not last long. The Portuguese fought a guerilla war until fresh troops arrived from Portugal and Spain. On March 29, 1625, an overpowering fleet of fifty Portuguese ships, with thousands of heavily armed men on board, sailed into the harbor at Bahia.

Soon Bahia was once more in Portuguese hands. Although the Portuguese promised safety to all the citizens of the city, five New Christians were executed for aiding the enemy during the Dutch occupation. Jews who had arrived from Holland were allowed to return, but no Portuguese Christians, Old or New, could now leave Bahia. Some, in fear for their lives, fled into the countryside.

Dutch plans for control of Brazil were reevaluated. Forced out of Bahia, the Dutch now looked to the northern province of Pernambuco. Conditions there were similar to those in Bahia: central location, good harbor, and a supportive Marrano population.

Even before the actual capture of Pernambuco, the members of the Dutch West India Company's board of directors, the Heeren XIX (Council of Nineteen), wrote a series of rules for the new colonies. Article Ten stated: "The liberty of Spaniards, Portuguese, and natives, whether they be Roman Catholic or Jews, will be respected. . . ."

When the Dutch captured Pernambuco on February 14, 1630, they renamed it Recife. Among those entering the conquered area were Moses Navarro, Samuel Cohen, and three other Jews. All were members of the Dutch army. These were the first Jewish soldiers in the New World. In short order the Dutch firmly established their rule over Recife. The Portuguese, however, continued to harass the settlement and its residents.

Marranos from Bahia made their way to the protection of Recife and used the promise of religious tolerance to publicly affirm their Judaism. Other Jews sailed from Holland to take advantage of the trade opportunities as well as the civil and religious freedoms of the colony. Slowly, an active and proud Jewish community began to emerge.

In 1636 a new governor was appointed by the directors of the Dutch West India Company. Johan Mauritz van Nassau was an enlightened man who provided the city with needed security and organization. He made Recife a cosmopolitan city that became a leading cultural and economic center in the New World.

Mauritz proved to be a popular leader. He introduced a legislative assembly to help him govern and set up a citizen militia to aid the army in protecting Recife. Included in that militia, for the first time ever in the New World, were Jewish residents of the community. In deference to their observance of the Sabbath, Jews were even excused from military service on Saturdays and Jewish holidays.

Yet despite these positive signs, anti-Jewish feelings still ran high among the general population. It upset the Old Christians in the Portuguese community to see the New Christians who once sat next to them in church now openly returned to Judaism. When, for example, Governor Mauritz received complaints from Christian clergy that Jews were holding loud public services, he ordered the Jews to limit their prayer services to private homes and to be as quiet as possible so as not to disturb Christians. Likewise, there were almost continuous complaints from Christian merchants about the competition from Jewish businesses.

But unlike conditions that prevailed against Jews in other countries of the world, here, as in Amsterdam, Jews were not afraid to speak up and request higher powers to overrule local officials. In Amsterdam, Jewish businessmen on the board of the Dutch West India Company exerted their influence in support of their brethren in Brazil.

It was, after all, in the best interests of the Dutch West India Company to support a business community that provided increasing profits. The result was even more Jewish emigration to Brazil. In 1638, a record two hundred Jews sailed from Holland to Recife. The city became known as the "port of the Jews."

Also in the Jews' favor was the fact that of all the residents of Brazil, they were the most loyal and supportive of Dutch rule. For the Jews it was a matter of survival. The return of Portuguese rule would certainly be accompanied by a form of the Inquisition. That loyalty was recognized by the officials in Holland, who continually prodded the local Dutch officials in Brazil to treat the Jewish community fairly.

In 1645, at the request of the leading Jewish residents of Amsterdam, special instructions reached the Supreme Council in Brazil concerning the situation of Jews in the colony. The message openly recognized the loyalty of the Jewish residents in Dutch Brazil. It was the first charter for Jews in the New World. "The Jews were to be protected from any damage to person or property in the same manner as were all the citizens of the United Netherlands." In the seventeenth century this was a unique statement for a Christian nation to make.

That same year saw the arrival of Jewish professionals in Recife with full permission to actively practice their skills. Michael Cardoso was the first Jewish attorney in the New World, Dr. Abraham de

Rabbi Isaac Aboab da Fonseca, the first rabbi in the New World. *Courtesy American Jewish Historical Society.*

Mercado the first physician and pharmacist, and Balthasar da Fonseca the first engineer, specializing in bridge building.

As the number of Jews in Recife grew, so did their religious and cultural needs. Although their first religious services were held in private homes, by 1638 synagogues were established in Recife and in the neighboring city of Mauricia.

The major congregation founded in Recife was called Zur Israel (Rock of Israel). It served as the center of Jewish communal life for all the Jews of Dutch Brazil. As in all Jewish communities, the members first established their own cemetery (at a distance from the city) and built two religious schools next to the synagogue. Soon the street in which these buildings stood became known as Rua dos Judeos (Street of the Jews).

In 1642 a large group of immigrant Jews arrived from Holland. Among the newcomers was the first rabbi in the New World, Isaac Aboab da Fonseca, one of the religious leaders of Amsterdam, who himself had been born into a Portuguese New Christian family. Accompanying him was a cantor, or prayer leader, Raphael Moses de Aguilar.

The congregation of Recife adopted rules and regulations for its members modeled after those of the richly developed Amsterdam Jewish community. Similar regulations were later adopted by congregations founded in New York and Newport. Leadership was in the hands of a five-member elected group known as the Mahamad. The members adopted a series of forty-two specific regulations that affected every Jew in Dutch Brazil.

Through these rules a system of social welfare and religious and community life was established. The group collected money to support needy Jews in the Holy Land and supervised the religious education of the young. To finance these community activities, the

Mahamad collected taxes from all the Jewish merchants of Brazil based on the amount of business each did. Voluntary contributions were encouraged.

The Mahamad was equally concerned with the relationships between Jews and non-Jews in the colony. Out of a total population in Recife of 12,700 about 1,450 were Jewish. One of the regulations prohibited Jews from engaging in religious disputes with non-Jews in order not to inflame emotions.

Whenever an individual Jew did something wrong, the entire Jewish community went to his aid—not necessarily because they liked him but to preserve the good name of the entire Jewish people. When one businessman committed suicide owing huge debts to non-Jewish merchants, the community made a special collection of money to repay what was owed.

The international political scene changed in 1640 when Portugal achieved independence from Spain. Although Holland and Portugal then entered into a joint treaty against Spain, conditions in the New World remained unclear. Governor Mauritz, for example, hurriedly used military force to increase the size of Dutch territory in Brazil before a formal truce could be signed with the Portuguese in Bahia.

In this uncertain peace, frequent military skirmishes took place between the Dutch and Portuguese in Brazil. The violence intensified and on June 19, 1645, the Dutch withdrew the rule that excused Jews from serving in the militia on the Sabbath. All residents of Recife were needed to stand guard against the Portuguese who were gradually encircling the city. Jewish residents not only willingly served as soldiers but contributed needed funds to support the government.

By 1646 Recife was under a nearly total siege by Portuguese

troops. Conditions within the city worsened. By then, the Jewish population had decreased to less than eight hundred. Many had returned to Holland. Others had died of hunger and rampant disease.

On June 11, 1646, strict rationing of oil and wine was imposed. Limited amounts of bread were distributed once a week. The only hope was from the sea, but no ships from Holland were seen on the horizon. Desperate, the Dutch decided that with food supplies gone, they would risk an armed breakout through the heavily defended enemy lines. Many would die, but there was nothing else to do. The residents of Recife were frightened and hopeless. They prayed for a miracle.

On June 23, 1646, to everyone's great surprise and relief, two Dutch ships were suddenly spotted making their way into the harbor. The unfurled sails of the *Elizabeth* and the *Valk* were a wonderful sight to the weakened citizens of Recife. Many, too tired to walk, crawled toward the harbor just to glimpse the two ships that had come to save them from death.

Like their fellow citizens, the Jews were eternally grateful. The Mahamad organized a religious service and declared that date in the Hebrew calendar a day of thanksgiving to be observed each year. Rabbi Aboab sat down at his desk and composed a special poem of thanks, which became the first piece of Hebrew literature written in the New World.

Although the community was saved from starvation, the siege and harassment by the Portuguese continued. Even the arrival of fresh troops from Holland could not prevent the shrinking in size of Dutch-held territory. When Dutch forces attempted a desperate military breakthrough, their forces were heavily defeated.

Amid growing food shortages and other dangers, Jews suffered even greater tragedy. To the Portuguese, these Jews were not Dutch citizens but Portuguese renegades to be hanged. While captured Dutch citizens who were not Jewish were treated humanely as prisoners of war, Jews were killed or shipped back to Lisbon for trial by the Inquisition. Although the Dutch objected directly to King Joao IV of Portugal about this unfair treatment, their efforts were in vain.

The case of Isaac de Castro created a great deal of furor. Castro was twenty-two years old when he was brought before the tribunal in Lisbon in 1647. The former Portuguese New Christian returned to Judaism when he settled in Dutch Brazil in 1641. On an ill-timed trip to Bahia, he was arrested by Portuguese authorities and turned over to the Inquisition. Although Church officials tried to convince him to return to Christianity, Castro was unmoved. The Dutch intervened on his behalf with the Portuguese Inquisition, but to no avail. He died at the stake confirming his Judaism.

Conditions continued to worsen in Recife. Food shortages, low morale, and military attacks became a way of life, and in February 1649 the Dutch were defeated when more than eight hundred soldiers died. Yet the end did not come quickly.

Although Recife was firmly surrounded by the Portuguese on land, sea access from Holland was still possible and the city was able to survive on the meager supplies shipped across the Atlantic. Then even that supply route shut down in 1651 as the Dutch were forced to assign all available ships to protect their home country from England, with which it was at war. All the while, negotiations continued in Europe toward the resolution of the political and military problems of the Dutch in Brazil.

There was no doubt that the Dutch presence in Brazil was drawing to a disastrous end. Yet Dutch officials wanted to ensure that their citizens—all citizens—would be treated fairly and honorably by the Portuguese. Finally, an agreement was reached. The official surrender took place on January 26, 1654, at 11:00 P.M.

The Portuguese commander, General Francisco Barreto, was a true gentleman. He quickly agreed that any Jews who had never been baptized could choose to remain in Brazil. Residents of Dutch Brazil who did not wish to live under Portuguese rule—and that included all the Jews and Marranos—were given three months to leave the country. Property had to be sold, businesses transferred, baggage packed, and passage booked on whatever ships could be found. It was a time of terrible anxiety.

By 1654 the Jewish population was down to about six hundred men, women, and children. Most decided to return to Holland. From there some moved on to England to become part of a growing Jewish community. Others eventually returned to the New World, where they settled on Caribbean islands under Dutch or English rule. Soon, vibrant Jewish communities existed in Barbados, Surinam, and Curaçao.

One group of Jews who set out for Holland never made it across the Atlantic. After a harrowing storm-tossed voyage from Recife, they were forced to land on Spanish territory in Jamaica. Those passengers who had been born Christian were detained by the authorities for investigation while the Jewish refugees were allowed to leave. This group quickly left Jamaica for the busy port of Cape Saint Anthony in nearby Cuba. There they hoped to find passage to the safety of a Dutch colony.

With nearly all their funds used up, they booked passage on a French ship bound for New Amsterdam, a Dutch West India Company colony today called New York City. There, they expected funds from Amsterdam to reach them with which to pay the captain.

71

In early September 1654 the *Sainte Catherine* entered the harbor of New Amsterdam. Nearly penniless, weary from the hazardous journey, and uncertain of their welcome in this new land, the Jewish passengers stepped hesitantly onto the soil of this Dutch territory. The history of the Jews in the United States begins with these twenty-three souls and their quest for religious and civil rights.

EIGHT

Finally, Freedom

"Giving them liberty, we cannot refuse the Lutherans and Papists."

GOVERNOR PETER STUYVESANT, 1655

Jacques de la Motthe was angry. The funds expected by the twenty-three Jews he had just transported from Cuba had not arrived. As master of the French ship *Sainte Catherine,* he now went into court at New Amsterdam to demand immediate payment.

The passengers claimed that the money was on the way from Amsterdam, but de la Motthe could not wait. The court ordered the belongings of all twenty-three passengers sold at auction. Two of the passengers were held in jail. Such was the beginning of the first Jewish community in North America.

These were not the only Jews on the continent. Elias Legardo had arrived in the colony of Virginia in 1621. In 1656, "ye Jew doctor" Jacob Lumbrozo settled in Maryland. Others Jews soon followed. Over the years these individual Jews had come to trade or to settle in many of the Dutch, English, and French colonies.

Peter Stuyvesant, governor of New Amsterdam from 1647 to 1664.
Courtesy New York Public Library Picture Collection.

Finally, Freedom

For about one hundred years after Columbus's discovery of the New World there were no real settlements in North America. In the early 1600s, companies were formed in Europe to send colonists across the Atlantic to settle and to organize trade. On May 13, 1607, three ships of the Virginia Company of England reached James- town, to found the first permanent English settlement in the New World.

Gradually others came and small settlements sprouted up and down the Atlantic coast. Some settlers, like those in Virginia, came for adventure and profit. Others, like the Puritans who landed on Plymouth Rock in 1620, came to escape religious persecution in England. Swedes and Finns came in 1638 and established small trading settlements along the Delaware River.

By 1626 the colony established in New Amsterdam by the Dutch West India Company was already flourishing, perhaps the best-prepared and -equipped colony on the continent.

Until the 1650s there were probably fewer than fifty widely scattered Jews in all of North America. They came as individuals not directly interested in establishing Jewish communities. In fact, two Jewish businessmen, Solomon Pietersen and Jacob Barsimson, were already in New Amsterdam when the *Sainte Catherine* docked. Barsimson was an "old-timer" who had arrived on business about two weeks earlier from Holland on board *de Pereboom* (the *Peartree*).

The governor of New Amsterdam was a tough-minded, flinty man with a wooden leg—Peter Stuyvesant. As the representative of the Dutch West India Company, Stuyvesant's role was to maintain law and order in the colony while encouraging trade to enrich the Company. He was not at all pleased with the arrival of twenty-three poor Jews.

Supporting the governor were the Dutch Reformed clergy.

75

Domine Johannes Megapolensis complained: "For as we have Papists, Mennonites and Lutherans among the Dutch: also many Puritans and Independents, and many atheists . . . it would create a still greater confusion if the obstinate and immovable Jews came to settle here."

Writing immediately to the directors of the Company in Amsterdam, Stuyvesant clearly stated his objections to Jews and asked permission to prohibit any further Jewish arrivals. Referring to Jews as "repugnant" and a "deceitful race," Stuyvesant also feared that the colony would have to support the poor refugees. "We have, for the benefit of this weak and newly developing place and the land in general, deemed it useful to require them in a friendly way to depart."

But the refugees also wrote letters—to their friends and relatives in Holland, many of whom were wealthy merchants and shareholders in the Dutch West India Company. These well-to-do residents of Amsterdam then sent a petition to the directors of the Company in January 1655 on behalf of the Jews in New Amsterdam. The petition referred to the sacrifices made by the Jews of Recife as well as to the loyalty shown the Dutch by Jewish inhabitants wherever they lived. The petition also reminded the directors that the Company had invited people to come and settle in the Dutch colonies of the New World.

> It is well known to your Honors that the Jewish nation in Brazil have at all times been faithful and have striven to guard and maintain that place, risking for that purpose their possessions and their blood.
>
> Yonder land is extensive and spacious. The more of loyal people that go to live there, the better it is in regard to the population of the country. . . .

Your Honors should also please consider that many of the Jewish nation are principal shareholders in the Company.

Meanwhile, Governor Stuyvesant left New Amsterdam to attend to urgent business elsewhere. Upon his return in July, he found a letter from the Company dated April 26, 1655. The instructions overruled all the governor's objections and granted the Jews official recognition. "These people may travel and trade to and in New Netherland and live and remain there, provided the poor among them shall not become a burden to the Company or to the community, but be supported by their own nation." The attitude of the Company was clear. Soon other Jews began arriving directly from Holland.

This was not to be the last correspondence about Jews between Stuyvesant and his superiors in Holland. Although the directors in Amsterdam supported the settlement of Jews in their colonies, many of the local officials, including Governor Stuyvesant, reflected the ingrained European anti-Semitism of the general population.

But unlike the Spanish and Portuguese, the Dutch were not obsessed by matters of religion. They were a merchant nation whose concern for trade and profit overrode religious zeal. While Jews and Christian denominations other than the Dutch Reformed Church were not at first allowed to build their own houses of worship, they were not prohibited from practicing their religions in private. The first Jewish congregation in North America, Shearith Israel (Remnant of Israel), dates its beginnings to April 26, 1655. The Dutch showed their tolerance by excusing Jews from appearing before the court on the Sabbath.

Yet these Jewish refugees were not content just to live according to selective rights handed to them. From the very beginning they insisted on and ultimately received the same rights and benefits accorded to other residents.

When Peter Stuyvesant continued reading his mail from Amsterdam, he found orders directing him to assemble a military force to attack Swedish positions on the Delaware River. The question now arose whether or not to include Jewish men in the militia. When the dilemma was brought before the governing Council, the answer was no surprise.

"That owing to the disgust and unwillingness of the trainbands [militiamen] to be fellow soldiers . . . Jews cannot be permitted to serve as soldiers, but should be exempt." But the council also ruled that those exempt from military service should pay a monthly tax. While most Jews nodded and grumbled, one of them, Asser Levy, decided not to keep quiet anymore. Whereas Stuyvesant was biased and strict, Levy was proud and unafraid. It was inevitable that the two should clash.

On November 5, 1655, Levy presented a petition asking that he and Jacob Barsimson be allowed to stand guard duty like other citizens of New Amsterdam or be excused from paying the unfair tax. Again the response from the council was not unexpected; the request was denied. The response closed with a pointed message that basically told the two men that if they didn't like living there, they were free to leave!

Shortly thereafter, perhaps due to yet another order from the directors in Amsterdam, Levy began to stand guard as a member of the militia alongside the other men of New Amsterdam.

New Amsterdam was then a small fort on the tip of Manhattan Island. The inhabitants lived with the constant threat of attack from hostile Indians. To provide greater protection, Stuyvesant and his council decided to build a bigger defense wall around the settlement. To raise money for the construction, all residents were asked for contributions. The Jewish residents were taken advantage of and although they constituted only one-thirtieth of the total population, their "voluntary contribution" for the wall was one-twelfth of the total.

Stuyvesant again wrote to the directors in Holland. "To give liberty to the Jews will be very detrimental . . . giving them liberty, we cannot refuse the Lutherans and Papists."

The directors in Holland patiently responded by reminding Stuyvesant that Jews had every right to go to New Amsterdam and "there to enjoy the same liberty that is granted them in this country." Yet even in this message, the directors repeated that Jews could hold religious services only in private. Probably anticipating a future question from the Jews about increasing their religious freedoms, the directors ordered Stuyvesant to refer any such questions directly to Holland for response.

Stuyvesant, now clearly annoyed, responded to the directors that Jews had the same rights to trade as others but he drew the line at allowing them to practice "their abominable religion" in public. Then, referring to the role of Amsterdam Jews in determining policy in the colonies, he added, "What they may be able to obtain from your Honors time will tell."

Slowly the Jews began to settle in. They took advantage of the abundant trading opportunities and soon those who had arrived penniless had become successful merchants. But even in business they had to fight for rights granted automatically to other merchants. There was much money to be made in trade along the South River and at Fort Orange (now Albany). Yet these areas were closed to Jews. On November 29, 1655, a petition signed by Abraham de Lucena, Salvador Dandrada, and Jacob Cohen was presented to the

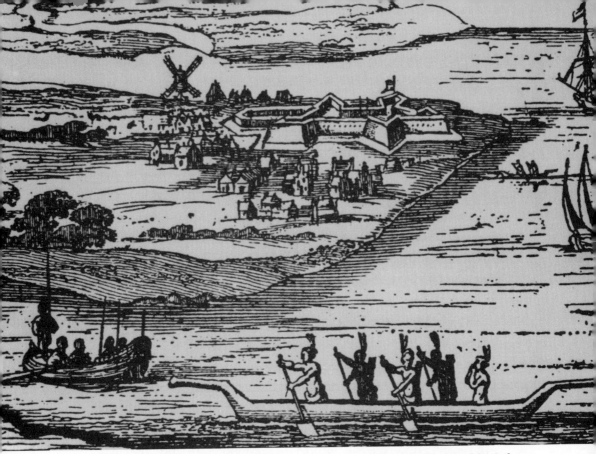

A scene of early New Amsterdam, 1625. *Courtesy New York Public Library Picture Collection.*

director general and the council seeking permission to trade, like any residents, anywhere within New Netherland, the province of which New Amsterdam was a part. Again came the usual response: No. However, since goods had already been shipped by the gentlemen to South River, they were allowed to send two people there to dispose of the merchandise and return directly to New Amsterdam.

In spite of these stumbling blocks to equality, the Jews felt secure enough in New Amsterdam to think of establishing a permanent community. Teunis Cray, a Dutchman, had a house for sale. Salvador Dandrada, a Jew, thought it would make a fine residence for himself and his family and offered to buy it. The only formality standing in the way of the sale was the approval of the council. On December 23, 1655, Dandrada submitted a petition seeking permission to purchase the house. His request was, of course, denied.

Cray was as upset as Dandrada; he had lost a sale. The angry Dutchman himself submitted a petition to the court. He demanded the sale be allowed or that the council pay the 1,860 guilders he would lose. The original answer to Dandrada remained unchanged and the house was later reoffered at auction.

Again Jews of New Amsterdam turned to petition. In a letter dated March 14, 1656, they described the previous petitions and made clear their demands for equality. One hundred twenty years before the Declaration of Independence, they called for no taxation without representation. ". . . [I]f, like other burghers, [Jews] must and shall contribute, [they must] enjoy the same liberty allowed to other burghers . . . in trading . . . as in the purchase of real estate."

Stuyvesant and the council answered coldly that the "contributions" were for the protection of all the inhabitants of New Amsterdam, including the Jews. As for their request to own real estate, the wary governor sent yet another message to the directors in Amsterdam.

By now, the directors were more than a little annoyed with their governor in New Amsterdam. "We have seen and learned with displeasure" his denial of trading rights to Jews, they wrote to Stuyvesant and the council. Further, ". . . we wish that this had not occurred but that your Honors had obeyed our orders which you must hereafter execute punctually and with more respect."

With more people coming to settle in New Netherland, the local inhabitants feared a loss in profits if others also had trading rights. On April 9, 1657, the *Burgomasters* (mayors) issued notice that all *burghers* (full citizens) must register and that within a short period of time only those holding burgher certificates would be allowed to continue trading. There were several classes of residents in the colony. Membership in the highest class, the burgher, entitled the holder to specific benefits not available to a general resident. Jews were merely residents and not entitled to the "burgher right."

Seeing yet another injustice, Asser Levy again appeared in court. He appeared before the judges with great frequency, taking advantage of the legal system to assert his rights as a businessman, citizen, and Jew. This time he calmly made a request to be granted the burgher right. After all, he could claim to have held that right in Amsterdam, where he previously resided. Now as a resident of New Amsterdam he regularly stood guard with other burghers in the militia, another right he had fought hard to achieve.

"Not allowed," responded the court. He was advised to address Stuyvesant and the council directly. This he did at once and was joined in the appeal by the other Jews of New Amsterdam.

With a resigned air, in a response dated April 20, 1657, Stuyvesant granted the petition of the Jews. Within the short space of three years, the Jews of New Amsterdam had risen from the status of unwelcome refugee to that of equal citizen.

Perhaps "almost equal citizen" would be more correct. Although Jews had built houses of worship in Amsterdam and Recife, they still were not allowed to build a synagogue in New Amsterdam. Nor were they permitted to engage in certain trades and crafts open to others. Asser Levy, however, did manage to obtain appointment as a butcher. In a twist of irony, his permit stated that he was excused from slaughtering pigs, a nonkosher animal!

Asser Levy was not afraid to stand up for the rights due him and his fellow Jewish citizens. His Christian neighbors respected his honesty and sought out his advice. His stubborn insistence on fair treatment helped establish the American tradition of equal rights for all. By the time he died in 1680, the Jewish community was firmly established on American soil.

The tolerance of the Dutch, despite a less than willing local attitude, set the tone for the tradition of religious liberty in North America. This attitude can be summarized in the 1663 response Stuyvesant received from the directors in Holland in the case of a Quaker seeking rights. "You may therefore shut your eyes, at least not force people's consciences but allow every one to have his own belief as long as he behaves quietly and legally, gives no offense to his neighbors, and does not oppose the government."

When New Amsterdam fell to the British in 1664 and became New York, nothing much changed for the inhabitants. Jews had always sought to emigrate to either Dutch or English colonies—both governments practiced a similar tolerance of religious differences.

Yet in English New York, as in Dutch New Amsterdam, no permission was forthcoming for the building of a synagogue. In 1685, when the Jewish community petitioned the British royal governor for permission, the royal answer, this time in English, not Dutch, was a firm no. The Lutherans fared better. In 1671 they were granted permission to build a church. As a sign of the generally good relations between Jews and Christians, funds for construction of the church were lent by the now wealthy Asser Levy.

Finally, in 1695, with permission from the Duke of York, Jewish worship moved from private homes to a simple house on Mill Street rented from David Provost for eight pounds a year. Old maps of that period clearly show the location of "the Jews synagogue." It was not until 1728 that the Jewish community was allowed to construct a proper synagogue for Congregation Shearith Israel.

The establishment of that synagogue near Mr. Provost's old

wood-frame house on Mill Street was a milestone in American religious history. The building was not impressive to look at: it was just
thirty-five feet long and twenty-one feet high. But its presence as a
publicly visible house of worship brought a sense of pride and satis-
faction to the small Jewish community.

Today, after several other moves, Congregation Shearith Israel
in the City of New York, the oldest Jewish congregation in the
United States, lives on in a magnificent building on Central Park
West in the heart of Manhattan. Within its walls can be found
many of the furnishings once contained in the original Mill Street
building. Twice a year, special prayers are still offered in recognition
of the contributions made by the Sephardic congregations of Curaçao, London, and Surinam in building and furnishing the original
synagogue, which was dedicated in 1729.

Modeled after the Sephardic congregation in Amsterdam, as
was Congregation Zur Israel in Recife, Shearith Israel quickly became the center of Jewish religious authority in North America and,
in turn, a model for synagogues established later on American soil.

The congregation quickly evolved into a uniquely American
institution. Interestingly, while Portuguese was the first official language of record, it didn't take long for the use of English to become
standard. To later Ashkenazic immigrant groups, the orderly worship
service and "Americanized" customs of Shearith Israel represented a
refreshing change from the rigid religious practices of European
ghettoes.

The descendants of Marranos survived as Jews over the centuries by having flexible attitudes. They fit in well with their Christian neighbors while successfully coexisting in a world of religious
and cultural differences.

By the start of the War of Independence there were about 2,500

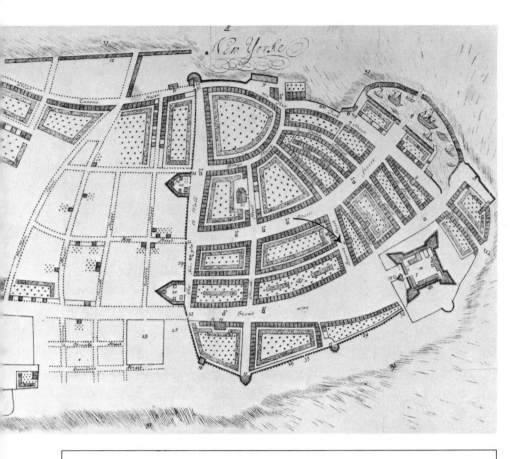

1.	The chappel in the fort of New-York	17.	The works on the west side of the city
2.	Leyster's half moon	18.	The north-west blockhouse
3.	Whitehall battery of 15 guns	19.	The Lutheran church and minister's house
4.	The old dock	20.	The stone points on the north side of the city
5.	The cage and stocks	21.	The Dutch Calvinist church, built 1692
6.	Stadthouse battery of 5 guns	22.	The Dutch Calvinist minister's house
7.	The stadt- (or state) house	23.	The burying ground
8.	The custom house	24.	A windmill
8.	The Bridge	25.	The King's farm
9.	Burghers, or the slip battery of 10 guns	26.	Coll. Dungan's garden
10.	The fly blockhouse and half moon	27.	Wells
11.	The slaughter-houses	28.	The plat of ground designed for the E. minister's house
12.	The new docks	29.	The stockade, with a bank of earth on the inside
13.	The French church	30.	The ground proper for the building an E. church
14.	The Jews synagogue	31.	Shewing the sea flowing about N. York
15.	The fort well and pump	32.	The city gates
16.	Ellet's Alley	33.	A postern gate

A 1695 map of New York showing "The Jews synagogue" as number 14. *Courtesy Map Division, The New York Public Library. Astor, Lenox, and Tilden Foundations.*

An early view of the Touro Synagogue in Newport, Rhode Island. Today it is a National Historic Site. *Courtesy American Jewish Historical Society.*

Jews in the Colonies. Jewish communities existed in Philadelphia, Charleston, Savannah, and New Orleans. The most important Jewish settlement outside of New York was in Newport, Rhode Island.

The first Jews arrived in Newport in 1658. In 1763 a synagogue for Congregation Yeshuat Israel (Salvation of Israel) was consecrated. The simple yet striking building was designed by the noted English architect, Peter Harrison. It stands today as the oldest continuously operating synagogue building in North America and is today a National Historic Site. It is called the Touro Synagogue, after Judah

Touro, the charitable and successful Jewish merchant who helped finance its construction.

A reminder of the past was built into it. Located near the pulpit is a secret trap-door leading to an escape tunnel—a remembrance of the dangerous life led by the congregation's Marrano ancestors. In America, the trap-door escape route was never needed.

When Henry Wadsworth Longfellow visited Newport and its synagogue he was moved to write his well-known poem "The Jewish Cemetery at Newport."

> The very names recorded here are strange,
> Of foreign accent, and of different climes;
> Alvares and Rivera interchange
> With Abraham and Jacob of old times.

The Jews in pre-Revolutionary America engaged in all manner of crafts and trades, from silversmith to merchant. Aaron Lopez became one of the wealthiest businessmen of his time. Jacob Rodriguez Rivera invented the sperm-oil lamp, an efficient lighting device, which led to the incredible growth of the American whaling industry. These men were not only involved in community life but took an active role in the heady politics of the time.

When the War of Independence began in 1776, American Jews drew sides as did their fellow countrymen. Most supported independence. Jews fought alongside their neighbors in that war as in all wars since.

The rabbi of Shearith Israel during that period was Gershom Mendes Seixas, an American patriot. With the British closing in on New York, some members of the congregation, along with the rabbi, gathered the ritual artifacts of the synagogue, including a Torah scroll, and fled the city. This was a clear message to the British and their supporters that this representative group of American Jews supported the Revolution and its ideals of liberty and freedom.

At the inauguration of George Washington as first president of the United States of America, Rabbi Seixas was one of thirteen invited clergymen. His influence extended beyond the Jewish community to include personal friendships with Christian clergy. He was the first Jewish-American appointed a trustee of Columbia University.

One young officer who fought under General Washington was named Asser Levy. He was the grandson of the man who, a century before, first won the right for American Jews to fight for freedom alongside other citizens.

NINE

Long Live Columbus

"The Government of the United States . . . gives to
bigotry no sanction, to persecution no assistance . . ."

GEORGE WASHINGTON TO THE JEWISH
CITIZENS OF NEWPORT

The Expulsion from Spain in 1492 was but one of many tragedies
to befall the Jewish people. Yet the memory of that disaster
scarred the Jewish mind forever. In spite of the sadness and personal
anguish of that event, one direct positive outcome was the eventual
establishment of the first thriving Jewish community in the United
States.

From the original twenty-three in 1654, the number of Jews in
the United States today stands at six million, the largest Jewish population of any country in the world—including Israel. The number
claiming Sephardic ancestry is quite small. The majority of Jews in
the United States today trace their ancestry to the two major waves
of emigration that began in 1848 and 1881, mainly from Russia,
Poland, and other East European countries.

Yet the presence and success of the proud Jewish population in America must be credited to the bravery, devotion, or perhaps luck of the original Jewish settlers of Spanish and Portuguese heritage.

In nature, the wind carries seeds of flowers and plants great distances. Yet there is no assurance of just how many will find the right conditions of climate and soil to ensure healthy, productive growth. The scattering of the Marranos and Jews of Spain to the countries of the world did not offer any guarantee of cultural survival. The arrival of those first Sephardic Jews in the New World appears to be only a fortunate accident of history.

In 1915 a Jewish engineer from Poland, on assignment in a remote part of Portugal, made a curious discovery. In the village of Belmonte he found residents who seemed to display uniquely Jewish practices. On further investigation, he learned that these simple villagers were really secret Jews.

Although they were practicing Christians, behind closed doors they observed certain customs and traditions that could only have come from the Jewish religion. They were direct descendants of Marranos, Jews who converted to Catholicism five hundred years earlier. The Marranos of Belmonte observed the Sabbath by not eating pork on Friday evenings and lighting specially made candles which were secretly placed in earthenware jars. They knew no Hebrew except for a few garbled words passed down through the generations. On Passover, however, they refrained from work and baked their own form of matzohs (unleavened bread).

Although they tried to keep their true beliefs hidden, neighbors openly referred to them as Jews. Dr. Joachim Prinz, in his book *The Secret Jews*, describes these hidden Jews. "The Marranos of Belmonte are still afraid. The timetable of their terrible, unshakable memories is very old: 1391, the slaughter of Seville: 1405, the bloodbath of Toledo: 1492, the expulsion from Spain: 1497, the massacre of Lisbon. Yet the memories of all these events are very much alive in the mountains of Portugal." Amazingly, these secret Jews could not believe that any other Jews still existed in the world!

These modern-day Marranos provide us with a glimpse backward to the past. How difficult and dangerous it must have been for their ancestors to pass down to the next generation even a small spark of Jewish heritage.

Today in communities as far apart as Spain, Portugal, South America, and Mexico, other descendants of Marranos live their normal lives. To themselves and to their neighbors they are exemplary Catholics, devoted to the Church in deed and in fact. Yet, without realizing the significance of their actions, many continue to practice traditions that mark them as descendants of Jews. When asked about these practices they have no explanation other than to say that is what their parents taught them. They know nothing of Jews or their own relation to the course of Jewish history. One estimate places the level of Jewish ancestry of today's Spanish citizens at thirty percent; of Portuguese, fifty percent.

Professor Yosef Yerushalmi, an expert on Marrano history, explains: "Marranos were a powerful testimony to the Jewish will to survive and to the essential resilience of the Jewish religion. Today there are Marranos in Spain whose ancestors were Marranos who converted in 1497. We should ask ourselves how powerful that flame must have been five centuries ago if they are still with us. Even the pathetic numbers that remain are testimony to this resilience of Judaism as a religion."

Other Jews also did what they could to ensure the survival of their heritage, religion, and culture. Luis de Santangel and Isaac Abravanel must have sensed something more in Columbus's plans than a money-making proposition.

The course of history might easily have been changed, as we

can see by the use of a simple two-letter word: *if*. We can only imagine what the Jewish world would be like today had only one of the following *ifs* happened:

> If Luis de Santangel and Don Isaac Abravanel had not been influential members of Ferdinand and Isabella's court.
>
> If Spain had not expelled the Jews from its territory.
>
> If religious bigotry had not forced the conversion of Jews.
>
> If the Portuguese had not claimed Brazil.
>
> If the Dutch had not welcomed the Jews to Recife.
>
> If the Portuguese had not reconquered Brazil.
>
> If the *Valk* had made a successful journey to Holland in 1654.
>
> If the twenty-three Jews had given in to Governor Stuyvesant's bigotry and left New Amsterdam.
>
> And finally, if Columbus had not made it possible for Jews and Marranos to find an "escape hatch" to the New World.

The year 1492 was an eventful one. For the Spaniards, it signified joy—the unification of their country under Catholic rule. For Columbus, it signified fulfillment—his discovery of the New World. For the Jews, it signified disaster—expulsion from a land they had called home for centuries.

At the time no one could realize how the three seemingly unrelated events of 1492 would dramatically become important chapters of the same story.

Later Jewish immigrants to America were no less thankful to Columbus than were the original refugees from Recife. The title of a popular Yiddish song sums up the gratitude felt by generations of American Jews: *Leben Zoll Columbus!*—Long Live Columbus!

A Select Bibliography

BOOKS

Ashtor, Eliyahu. *The Jews of Moslem Spain*, 2 vols. Philadelphia: The Jewish Publication Society, 1979.

Baer, Yitzhak. A *History of the Jews in Christian Spain*, 2 vols. Philadelphia: The Jewish Publication Society, 1978.

Bendiner, Elmer. *The Rise and Fall of Paradise*. New York: Putnam, 1983.

Eban, Abba. *Heritage: Civilization and the Jews*. New York: Summit, 1984.

Granzotto, Gianni. *Christopher Columbus*. Garden City: Doubleday, 1985.

Grayzel, Solomon. A *History of the Jews*. Philadelphia: The Jewish Publication Society, 1968.

Lebeson, Anita Libman. *Pilgrim People*. New York: Harper, 1950. (O.P.)

Liebman, Seymour B. *The Jews in New Spain*. Coral Gables, Florida: University of Miami Press, 1970.

Marcus, Jacob R. *Early American Jewry, 1649–1794*. Philadelphia: The Jewish Publication Society, 1951.

95

Marcus, Jacob R. *The Jew in the Medieval World*. New York: Atheneum, 1983.

Marcu, Valeriu. *The Expulsion of the Jews from Spain*. New York: The Viking Press, 1935.

Netanyahu, B. *Don Isaac Abravanel*. Philadelphia: The Jewish Publication Society, 1982.

Pool, David de Sola. *The Mill Street Synagogue*. New York: Congregation Shearith Israel, 1930. (O.P.)

Prinz, Joachim. *The Secret Jews*. New York: Random House, 1973.

Roth, Cecil. *Dona Gracia of the House of Nasi*. Philadelphia: The Jewish Publication Society, 1948.

Roth, Cecil. *A History of the Marranos*. New York: Schocken, 1974.

Wiznitzer, Arnold. *Jews in Colonial Brazil*. New York: Columbia University Press, 1960.

ARTICLES

Dyer, Albion. "Site of the First Synagogue of the Congregation Shearith Israel of New York." *Publications of the American Jewish Historical Society*, No. 8, 1900.

Huhner, Leon. "Asser Levy." *Publications of the American Jewish Historical Society*, No. 8, 1900.

Oppenheim, Samuel. "The First Settlement of the Jews in Newport." *Publications of the American Jewish Historical Society*, No. 34, 1937.

Oppenheim, Samuel, "The Early History of Jews in New York, 1654–1664." *Publications of the American Jewish Historical Society*, No. 18, 1909.

Wiznitzer, Arnold. "The Exodus from Brazil and Arrival in New Amsterdam of the Jewish Pilgrim Fathers, 1654." *Publications of the American Jewish Historical Society*, No. 54, 1954.

Index

Index

INDEX